Climbing
KILIMANJARO
At 70

Best Wishes

Dick Wolfe

Other Publications by
Dr. Richard A. Wolfe

History of the Coal Industry between 1900 and 2000

Published short stories and articles include:

"Sport and the Russian Black Pony Coat"
"Coal and the Legend of a Man called Sport";
"Sport and Bess—two families one marriage,
very different allegiances in the 'War between the States'"
"It's time to reawaken the 'sleeping giant' of America"
In addition, Dr. Wolfe has published over 100 articles
in peer-reviewed scientific publications pertaining to
clean energy and the environment.

For Bonnie + Daniel with love!
Merry Christmas
2010
Leigh + Billy

Climbing
KILIMANJARO
At 70

Richard A. Wolfe, Ph.D.

INGALLS
PUBLISHING GROUP, INC

2010

INGALLS PUBLISHING GROUP, INC

PO Box 2500
Banner Elk, NC 28604
www.ingallspublishinggroup.com

© Richard A. Wolfe, Ph.D.

Library of Congress Cataloging-in-Publication Data

Wolfe, Richard A., 1940-
Climbing Kilimanjaro at 70 / Richard A. Wolfe.
p. cm.
ISBN 978-1-932158-90-8 (trade pbk. : alk. paper)
1. Mountaineering--Tanzania--Kilimanjaro, Mount. 2. Kilimanjaro, Mount, Region (Tanzania)--Description and travel. 3. Wolfe, Richard A., 1940---Travel--Tanzania--Kilimanjaro, Mount. I. Title. II. Title: Climbing Kilimanjaro at seventy.
GV199.44.T342K559 2010
796.52'20967826--dc22
2010024431

Printed in the United States of America
November 2010

Dedication

For the three heroes in this book. Without their support and encouragement, I seriously doubt I could have made it to the summit of Mount Kilimanjaro.

To Dean Yates, my nephew and climbing partner.

To Atililo Juan Hemedi, my mountain guide who stayed with me to the summit and back.

To Coffee, my chocolate Labrador, who climbed every day with me for two years while training on Beech Mountain, North Carolina in all sorts of weather.

Table of Contents

Acknowledgments

This dream to climb to the summit of Mount Kilimanjaro started when I was seventeen and took me until I was 70 years old to achieve it. But I will never forget what my father always told me, "The turtle does not get on the fence post by itself." And neither did I climb Mount Kilimanjaro without a lot of support and encouragement from my family and friends.

I particularly appreciate the understanding and support from my wife, Dede Walton, who climbed many of the mountains with me during the past two years and continues hiking with me today. Dede heroically managed to keep our winery and inn business opened here in Banner Elk, North Carolina, while I was in Tanzania during the worst snow storm we have experienced in the past fifty years.

My two sons, Eric and Travis, although they could not go with me on this climb, were there with me in spirit and love.

I thank my old high school best friend, Dr. Buddy Thomas for prescribing a number of medicines to help keep me safe.

I would be remiss if I did not thank my two best friends: Mr. Pat Burdiss and Mr. Mike Moore of Beckley, West Virginia, who listened to me plot and plan this entire adventure over the past two years. Much of their wise council was taken—except when they said I was crazy for even attempting such an adventure at my age.

I wish to thank Bob Ingalls, of Ingalls Publishing Group, Inc, for stopping to chat with me when he saw me hiking these local mountains roads over the past two years in all sorts of weather. Little did I or he know, during those brief conversations, that I could make it to the summit of Mount Kilimanjaro. For if I had not made it to the summit, this book could have never been written by me or published by him.

Lastly, I thank Judith Geary for doing an excellent job of editing the book, while cleaning up my grammar and maintaining some of my West Virginia slang.

Preface

The Tanzanian tradition is that "Only the ones who have reached the summit of Mount Kilimanjaro can refer to that mountain as *Kili*." Having celebrated my 70th birthday on that mountain and reached the summit of Uhuru Peak at 8 a.m. on January 15, 2010, I suppose that I have earned that right. However, after having experienced the awe and difficulty of that mountain, I feel it is disrespectful to call it anything other than Mount Kilimanjaro.

Upon on my return from climbing Mount Kilimanjaro, a number of local newspaper reporters wanted to tell my story, particularly because of my age in climbing the fourth highest mountain in the world. Their comments were that I might inspire other seniors in their local areas to set goals and get in better physical shape.

As the preface to my own story, I have included these newspaper articles that give a summary of my mountain quest. These articles set the stage for me to write my own story, which is far more personal. Hopefully, my account will tell more about who I am as a person, and why I was able to achieve the summit of Mount Kilimanjaro.

Mr. Mike Owens, a reporter from the *Bristol Herald Courier*, knew that I was making an attempt to climb Mount Kilimanjaro on my 70th birthday and asked if I would give him an interview after I returned. The following story was published on the front page of that newspaper on February 1, 2010. Mr. Owens captured the moments of that climb almost as if he were there with me. With permission from the newspaper, I am including Mr. Owens' full story.

Mr. Frank Ruggiero, editor of the *Mountain Times* newspaper from Boone, North Carolina, also knew that I had been training for more than a year by climbing these local Appalachian Mountains and wanted to write an article for the High Country locals on my return. Included is his article as a result of my interview after returning from Africa.

In addition to the two above newspaper articles, the local newspaper in the town where I lived my early days in and around Beckley, West Virginia, also wanted to write an article. Mr. Chris Jackson's article is included, for he also captured the moment and the significance of this climb to the Roof of Africa. See the Appendix for the articles.

Wolfe on Kilin

Area man reaches summit at 70

By Frank Ruggiero

Like most adventures, Dick Wolfe's started in a cinema.

A noted chemist, Wolfe is known locally as the vintner and co-owner of the award-winning Banner Elk Winery. But 53 years ago, he was running a movie projector in Sophia, W.Va.

The film was *The Snows of Kilimanjaro*, starring Gregory Peck and Susan Hayward, based on Ernest Hemingway's short story.

"That was my eyes to the world," Wolfe said of the cinema, "and the first time I'd heard of Kilimanjaro. You have a quest sometimes, when you think, 'I can do this, and I can do that.' Mt. Kilimanjaro has always been mine since I was a teenager."

Decades later, Wolfe celebrated his 70th birthday in Tanzania, specifically Uhuru Peak, the highest summit of Mt. Kilimanjaro, at 19,341 feet above sea level – the tallest mountain in Africa, and the tallest freestanding mountain in the world.

"Like so many things, growing up in these (Appalachian) mountains gave me the chance to get to know these mountains," said Wolfe, who, as a child, would race 4 to 5 miles up and down the slopes. "I guess I've been preparing myself all my life."

The more intensive preparation came this past year, namely by hiking weekly to the summits of area slopes in Banner Elk and Beech Mountain, what Wolfe called "one of the better training grounds" for mountain ascensions.

Meanwhile, Wolfe's nephew, landscaper and Virginia Tech graduate Dean Yates, 36, who would accompany him on the expedition, trained in Abingdon, Va. Though nearly overwhelmed by Kilimanjaro's harsh climate, both were fully prepared, as were the 14 others in their 24-person expedition, divided into two groups,

Richard Wolfe and his ne

Mountain Empire

BY MICHAEL L. OWENS
BRISTOL HERALD COURIER

T t
70.

*R*ichard Wolfe didn't care about the air's icy bite: It was fresh – the purest he'd ever inhaled.

So what if a battle raged in his lungs – as the thin, mountain air fought for space against a dangerous fluid build-up? It took nearly a week of day-long hikes and nights in a sleeping bag to reach this point. He couldn't turn back now, not with the peak of Mount Kilimanjaro finally in sight.

Wolfe's pace slowed as he neared the 19,341-foot summit – more like shuffling forward than actual walking. Debilitating headaches and non-stop vomiting already had convinced others in the group to turn back. But Wolfe, continued upward, determined to reach Africa's highest peak.

Never mind that climbers have roughly five minutes to admire the serenity before more-severe symptoms of altitude sickness

Local bu
a few w
preparin
degree

set i

De
just
Cele
day
of th

Dr. Richard Wolfe, a native of Sophia, and his mountain climbing guide smil

ould have

reached
t, which is
er rim be-
was still

to walk
s, you got
to walk
id. "I said,
little be-
I'll make

ed if he
of 12 people and could make it to the
summit and he replied

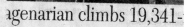

CONTRIBUTED PHOTO

and at the base of Mount Kilimanjaro.

OF KILIM

CONGRATULATIONS
YOU ARE NOW AT

PEAK TANZANIA 5895M

'S HIGHEST POINT
'S HIGHEST FREE-ST

ales fabled peak on 70th birthday

; *maybe, for others at*
le know it can be done.'
Richard Wolfe
the 19,341-foot summit of Mount Kilimanjaro

N.C., it is his search for clean-coal technology in Southwest Virginia that has grabbed local headlines in recent years.

Next on his to-do list is to write a book about his adventure, titled "Climbing Kilimanjaro at 70."

"I want to set the bar, maybe, for others at 70," Wolfe said. "I want to let people know it can be done."

Wolfe is not the oldest person to scale the inactive volcano in northeastern Tanzania, on the eastern side of the continent. In fact, there's a bit of contention over who holds that record, according to Climb Mount Kilimanjaro.com.

The Guinness Book of World Records bestows the distinction upon American Carl Haupt, who was 79 years old when he reached the top in 2004.

But many Web sites dedicated to the mountain credit a Frenchman named Valtee Daniel as the oldest

See **CLIMB**, Page **A3**

EARL NEIKIRK|BRISTOL HERALD COURIER

Wolfe climbed Mount Kilimanjaro
birthday. He spent a year
ached the summit in zero-
by his nephew, Dean Yates.

Getting there

Coal is how Wolfe is best known.

Though he operates a vineyard in Banner Elk,

agenarian climbs 19,341-

EARL NEIKIRK|BRISTOL HERALD CO

chard Wolfe displays a document from the
nzanian National Park service that certifies his
ek to the peak of Mount Kilimanjaro.

"It's super quiet," Wol

Climbing
KILIMANJARO
At 70

CHAPTER 1

Early Background

I grew up in the mountains of West Virginia in the small coal mining town of Sophia. Of course, as I ran up and down those hills and mountains, I had no way of knowing how those memories would come back and what they would mean to me as I faced the biggest mental and physical challenge of my life in climbing to the summit of the highest free-standing mountain in the world.

All of us kids who grew up in that small coal-mining town, walked and ran everywhere we went, including walking to both elementary and high school. Owning a car, or even driving, was out of the question as any car was used by our dads to go back and forth to the coal mines. It seemed nothing for us boys to walk across the mountain some eight or ten miles to swim or trout fish in the head waters of the Laurel Creek near another mining town of Pemberton. On several occasions, I have caught as many as twenty trout and then lugged them across the mountain to home in time for dinner. We thought nothing of walking ten miles to the top of Tams Mountain to hunt squirrels. On several occasions, I have lugged twelve or fifteen squirrels back home in time for dinner. My dad, Sport Wolfe as the other miners called him, was always surprised and pleased when I showed him how many trout or squirrels I had caught and killed. Mom, Bessie Wolfe, was a great cook and would always have a big Sunday dinner of squirrel and gravy or fried trout for the family—a family which usually included our Uncle Foggie and Aunt Lula and their five kids as well as many of our neighbors. Mom could take fifteen squirrels or twenty trout and feed the multitudes. And what pride it gave me to know that I was helping the family with the meals.

Dad also taught me to plant and care for a big garden during the summer. We would grow enough green beans, corn, potatoes, collards and other greens for Mom to can during the summer to last us all through the winter. In the fall, we would all gather hickory nuts and black walnuts so we could crack them for snacks while sitting around the fat-belly iron stove in the winter months. That stove was heated with coal that we had gathered from the nearby railroad tracks.

I related the above stories as examples of what it was like living and growing up in those West Virginia Mountains some seventy years ago. When we walked through the villages near Kilimanjaro and on the lower leg of the climb, I saw kids so much like I was at their age, gathering wood and grass to help their families. The photograph below shows some of those kids gathering wood as we started the climb on January 11, 2010, which brought back my own childhood memories in Sophia, West Virginia. It seemed that I had stepped back in time and was looking at myself and my friends gathering coal that had fallen off the rail cars and wood for many of the older ladies who needed heat and had little money and no one to help them. All of us kids were taught by our parents to help out at home and with our neighbors. That was just the way it was in those mountains of West Virginia and it is the same now in these villages surrounding Mount Kilimanjaro.

Dean Yates, my nephew, and myself on the first leg of the climb through the rain forest on the Rongai Route

My dad worked at the nearby coal mines in Affinity, West Virginia, some four miles away from Sophia. During the summers, particularly, I would walk to the coal mines so I could be there when he came out of the coal mines, usually around 4 p.m. After his bath, I could then ride back home with him, and he would tell me all about coal mining. Most often, I would get to the mines two to three hours early so I could watch the coal being pulled out of the mine by an electric motor car driven by a miner sitting down in the motor so low that you could just see the top of his head. The motor car usually pulled about twenty cars containing tons of coal piled high. The coal was then dumped on a beltline leading into a big building called a *tipple* where the coal was screened, crushed, and cleaned of some of its dirt and rock. It was fascinating to watch.

I learned first of all to stay out of the way so the miners would not get mad at me, for they all knew that I was Sport Wolfe's boy. That alone made me proud. In fact, one summer, I went to the mines so often that some of the miners would share their lunch with me. One particular

The young Dick Wolfe with his father, Sport Wolfe

miner, Mr.Farley, told me that I had been to the mines so often that I should get a pay check, and they gave me three dollars in an envelope with a note saying, "Not missed a day of work in the past 6 weeks." My dad was proud of me when he heard of my paycheck. It seemed that I was one of the few boys who showed interest in coal mining and the coal cleaning process.

And true enough, clean coal technology has become much of my life's work and still my passion for now over fifty years. In fact, on the Internet, if one types in on Google, "Richard Wolfe Coal Scientist," they can learn much about my quest for making coal a clean energy fuel. My dad died in 1968 of black lung disease when he was 67 years old. Since my dad's death, I have dedicated much of my professional life to developing clean coal technology. My latest invention in 2009 was developing a technology to remove 100 percent of the mercury from coal during a mild gasification process and reducing the overall emissions significantly when coal is burned in making electricity at the utility power plants.

I make mention of this early part of my life with my dad and the coal mines to make the point that we walked a lot and learned a lot around the coal mines that helped lead me to have a great appreciation of the mountains and their resources. As I toured the villages around Mt. Kilimanjaro before and after the climb, I saw so many kids and people working manually without modern machines and digging gardens and planting crops with the use of a donkey or an ox that it reminded me once again of my own early life some sixty years ago. Again, a step back in time makes me think about where Tanzania may be in the next sixty years.

Little did I know what those early years of my life were teaching and preparing me for—to appreciate the beauty of the mountains and to not be afraid of or intimidated by those lofty peaks. We boys would run for miles just to see who could get to the mountain top first. We would pretend to be Indians and follow some of the same trails through the forest that the early Native Americans traveled. It snowed often in winter in the West Virginia mountains, and nearly always we would have a White Christmas. All through my elementary and high school days, we looked forward to winter—cold weather and snow. All of us kids enjoyed riding our sleds from the top to the bottom of hills which could be as long as a mile down snow-covered roads, made slick as ice so no cars could get up the hills. The adults just parked their cars at the bottom of the hill and walked home. We would build fires, mostly from fallen wood and old tires, along the slopes so we could stop to get warm on the way down or on our hike back up to the top of the mountain. What thrills we had—and what a training ground for my later climb up Kilimanjaro.

The snows also brought rare beauty to our coal mining town. Snow covered the hills and all the black coal roads as if God had painted the dirty, dusty roads and houses with a canopy of white paint. For those three months of winter, it was a most magical, beautiful time —so different from the other nine months of the year with coal dust blowing everywhere covering the houses, roads, and cars with a dingy black dust. Seldom was school canceled because of snow, since we all walked to school anyway, as did many of the teachers. Sometimes, we would get temperatures below zero degrees Fahrenheit. and that was when us kids would huddle around the two or three fires strung out along the mountain sled paths to laugh, snow ball battle, and get warm by the open fire.

When I reached high school, although only 135 pounds, I played football, basketball, and baseball for our high school team. Now, granted, I sat on the bench most of the time. But I did have a uniform and got to play sometimes, mostly when the team was either far ahead or far behind. I could always run fast and had good hand-eye coordination, so in baseball games, I seldom ever struck out—mostly I hit grounders into the infield, but I got on base because I could run fast.

All these early experiences of living in the mountains of West Virginia prepared me with a love for adventure and the outdoors. However, my eyes to the world were really opened, when during my senior year of high school at the age of seventeen, I got a job at the local theatre running the projectors and showing movies every evening and on the weekends. My friend Chuck Smith had that job for several years and it was his dad who owned the theatre. Chuck trained me and then gave me his job when he went off to college.

The first I ever heard of Mount Kilimanjaro was when we showed that famous movie titled, *Snows of Kilimanjaro,* from the book written by Ernest Hemingway and starring Gregory Peck, Ava Gardner, and Susan Hayward. I learned that Kilimanjaro was located in Tanzania in Africa and was the fourth highest mountain in the world and the world's highest free-standing mountain. I must have watched that movie forty times and thought that I might like to go there sometime, but *sometime* looked a long way off. It turned out that showing all those different movies became my "eyes to the world." I saw what Rome looked like in *Three Coins in the Fountain*, and I saw Paris in *April in Paris*.

During these past seventy years, I have managed to visit most of the places that I first saw in those movies from around the world. One could say that first job in the local theater gave me a thirst for adventure and to travel. I can now say that this small boy growing up in the coal mining town of Sophia, West Virginia, has seen most of the great sights around the world. There are still a few sites that I have yet to visit, including the Pyramids of Egypt and the Acropolis in Athens, Greece. just to mention a few on my *Bucket List*. But I don't see myself having a desire to climb Mount Everest now that I am 70 and have experienced just how difficult it was to climb Mount Kilimanjaro.

As I look back on my early years of living in those mountains of West Virginia, I can see why I have always had a love for and an appreciation of the mountains and vistas from those high peaks. It is probably the reason that over these 70 years, I have always found my way back to the mountain atmosphere. It is no different now, with my living for the past nine years in these mountains of North Carolina around this little town of Banner Elk. Banner Elk is located in the valley between Sugar Mountain and Beech Mountain and is the ski capital of, not just North Carolina, but, arguably, the entire east coast of the United States. Banner Elk is a small town with one stop light and lies at 4000 feet elevation along the Eastern Continental Divide. The ski slopes of Sugar Mountain reach nearly 5100 feet and those of Beech Mountain reach 5500 feet, making them the highest slopes and town in the eastern United States. My house sits on the Banner Elk Winery vineyards at 4300 feet elevation at the base of Beech Mountain. The slopes outside my door reach all the way to the top of Beech Mountain. These local mountains became my daily training ground for the climb up Kilimanjaro. I felt that living now at 4300 feet and hiking these local mountains along my own paths as steep as I could find them would be one of the best training grounds that I could ever find. So, in November of 2008, I started the training of climbing and hiking as a daily route. See the photographs taken in November 2008, while hiking up Beech Mountain in the snow.

I figured out a route to hike different trails of varying difficulty, to keep the training interesting in all types of weather throughout the year. During winter, the temperatures and wind chill factor could get as low as -15°F. around Banner Elk, and in the summer, the temperatures could reach 85°F. These climate changes really reflected what we experienced during the climb up Kilimanjaro—first hiking through the rain forest at 90°F. and then through four more different climate zones finally reaching the Arctic Zone on the summit at nearly -20°F.

Training for the climb during November 2008, with my faithful dog companion Coffee

CHAPTER 2

Early Preparations
for Climbing Kilimanjaro

It seems amazing to me now, at 70, how many of our life's passions begin with a single event. For example, in the 1951-1952 period after World War II, the coal industry was in a big growth period, for America was rebuilding its industry, and coal was needed. Many of the mine operators, including my dad, were hiring new people coming from Europe. The Malino family, with a young daughter and two sons near my age of twelve, moved near our house in the town of Sophia. Other Italians also moved into town to help in mining coal. Before long, Mr. Malino brought some grape vines from Italy, and we all helped him plant a small vineyard of about 100 vines. The grapes did well, and soon we boys were picking grapes, stomping them, and helping Mr. Malino make some homemade wine. I was fascinated by the process of converting grapes into wine and began to learn as much as I could about the process from Mr. Malino and other Italians. It was there, at the age of twelve, that I developed my second passion of wine-making, second only to my first passion of clean coal technology.

I have now started growing grapes in the High Country of North Carolina and have encouraged and taught over 35 other farmers to grow wine grapes. We have built a major new winery called "Banner Elk Winery" in Banner Elk, North Carolina, and opened that winery in 2006. I had in mind to take a bottle of Banner Elk Wine on my Kilimanjaro adventure and toast the summit with a glass. However, I knew it was too heavy and dangerous to carry a glass wine bottle up that mountain, and I didn't even know for sure if I could make it to the summit. So I left that idea back at home. I did, however, wear my Banner Elk Winery t-shirt to the summit and unzipped my down jacket long enough to show it in the summit picture later in this book.

In 1956, a coal mine near Sophia had a mine explosion killing a number of my classmates' fathers. My dad escaped that mine disaster. As we talked during the months that followed, he explained that methane gas comes out of the coal as it is being mined. The miners use a safety lamp which has a small flame inside to detect that gas. As the flame burns higher with support from the methane gas, this becomes an indicator for the miners to get out of the mine before an explosive mixture develops. As Dad explained this process to me, he said, "The problem is you are in the middle of gas when you detect it and any spark will set off an explosion." He continued, "It is much like being in a nest of rattlesnakes when you hear them rattle."

In my simple mind, I thought there should be some way to detect the gas before it ever accumulates. So, I got this idea of setting safety lamps around the mine with an alarm system and indicator light to a control room outside the mines to warn miners when explosive methane gas was present. I developed the idea into a Science Project for the spring of 1957. I ended up winning first place in the Southern West Virginia Science Fair and fourth place in USA National Science Fair in Los Angeles, California. This national science fair award was instrumental in my obtaining a full scholarship to Virginia Tech to study engineering and relieving, greatly, the burden of my family providing my college expenses. My dad was so pleased, for he had always said, "Son, get yourself a good education and that is your ticket out of these coal fields."

In the fall of 1957, I went off to college, graduating in 1961 with a degree in Chemical Engineering from Virginia Tech in Blacksburg, Virginia. I accepted a position with the Monsanto Research Corporation at the Mound Laboratory in Miamisburg, Ohio. Mound Lab was a primary contractor with the US Atomic Energy Commission. This was a top secret position in which I was involved in working with nuclear weapons and on the Apollo Moon Mission Nuclear Energy Device. I knew immediately that my Chemical Engineering degree was not sufficient to understand all the advanced nuclear physics that I was being exposed to, so I entered night school in 1962 at the University of Cincinnati to obtain my Master of Science in Nuclear Engineering. After four years of taking two and three night classes a week, I earned my MS degree in 1966. Now that I had four years under my belt at driving to Cincinnati more than 100 miles per night, I said to myself,

"I can't stop now," and thought how proud Dad and Mom would be to know that their son would one day be called *Doctor*.

That same type of determination came over me when I reached the crater's edge at Gilman's Point at daylight on January 15, 2010. I said to myself, "I can't stop now." In fact, once I evaluated my physical condition and could see that I was thinking clearly without any headaches, and that only my chest was tight, which I thought was natural, I proceeded with some other climbers and our guide, Atilio, to go forward to the summit.

I still am motivated by that type of recognition of not giving up on something started which helped me scale Mount Kilimanjaro at 70. My dad would always tell me, "Son, once a task is begun, never leave until it is done. Be the labor great or small, do it well or not at all." I have tried to live by that saying all my life.

After another seven years at night school, I finally graduated with my doctorate in Nuclear Engineering in 1973 at the age of 33. My father lived to see me graduate with my master's degree, but died in November 1968, at the age of 67 from a heart attack caused by his black lung disease. He didn't live to see me obtain my Ph.D., but somehow I know that he knew his son, this son of a coal miner, could now be called *Doctor*. During the next six years, I worked in the nuclear energy field at the Monsanto Research Corporation and then joined the US Department of Energy (DOE) in 1974 in Washington, D.C., as a project manager in charge of developing safe methods to dispose of plutonium nuclear waste. The nuclear energy field became stalled in the USA in the late 1970s, and the need existed to convert coal into transportation fuels under President Carter's new program of energy independence. I then left the DOE to join United Coal Company in Bristol, Virginia, as Vice President of Research and Development. This was when I started to develop new and cleaner methods to mine and convert coal into transportation fuels much like had been done in South Africa with the SASOL Company. Now, for the past thirty years, I have concentrated my technical and management efforts in this area of clean coal technology. I hope to help develop and commercialize new technologies, so that we can use our vast coal resources in a clean environment to the betterment of mankind.

As I now reflect back upon our group of climbers on this Kilimanjaro mountain attempt, I realize that many, nearly half, were below the age of thirty. And then I think, *What I was doing at the age of thirty?* It is no wonder it has taken me seventy years to find the time to train and climb that mountain of my dream. Perhaps life requires some of us to take longer to achieve certain goals than others, but in reality it is always about selecting our own priorities.

Preparation for the Climb

I have always had a love of the mountains and have enjoyed finding and walking the original Indian trails beneath the canopy of these mountain forests. My love for hunting and fishing came natural since I lived among these mountains and my dad taught me at a young age to appreciate the wildlife and to hunt for our food. That joy of the outdoors has become my lifelong friend and I have continued going camping, hunting and fishing every year for the past thirty years in the Mount Rogers National Forest in Virginia. I took my two boys as well as Dean Yates, my nephew and Kilimanjaro climbing partner, on numerous hunting trips.

After my boys graduated from the university, they took jobs that did not allow them to join me many times on our annual hunting and fishing trip. Since Dean lives in Virginia, owns a nursery, and because of his own love for the mountains, he has joined this hunting group every year for the past 20 years. About fifteen years ago, Dean and I started having a trout fishing tournament between ourselves on the Sunday before opening day of hunting season started. The one who caught the least number of trout in a two-hour period had to clean all the trout. Well, the first few years, I out-fished Dean and he learned to clean fish. But that soon stopped abruptly because he became an expert trout fisherman and for the past ten years, I have cleaned trout every year. In fact, it was so bad that in November, 2008, as shown in the photograph, I caught one trout and Dean caught 25. Needless to say, we had one big fish fry and the hunting group had one big laugh at me cleaning all those trout.

For the past thirty years, my buddies, including my brother-in-law Tom and his son Dean and up to ten other friends, have met the third week in November for our annual hunting and fishing trip at the Grindstone Camp Ground in the Mount Rogers National Forest in Virginia. The campsite is within ten miles of the community of White Top Mountain.

Fishing in 2008 while on our annual deer hunting trip

We have climbed those mountains starting at 3 a.m. looking for those monstrous bucks, climbed through the snow in zero degree weather, sleeping in tents and in the back of our trucks. And we enjoy cooking and sitting around the open fires at night. Mount Rogers and White Top Mountain are in the highest mountain range in Virginia, averaging about 5500 feet in elevation. Dean and I found out years ago that we could not sleep in the warm camper with Tom, Joe, Jim and others, because those guys snored so much and so loud that we could not sleep. So, at first, I was the only one sleeping in my sleeping bag in a tent in the cold. After a few years, Dean agreed that he couldn't sleep with his dad either. So, we two have slept in tents or our vehicles for the past ten years. Sometimes, as much as ten inches of snow had fallen during the night on the vehicles and the temperature hovered around zero degrees. We had down-filled sleeping bags, and always we slept warm no matter what the temperature was outside. It was those same sleeping bags that we took to Kilimanjaro and we slept warm each night on the climb.

After hunting one Saturday morning in 2008, Dean and I decided to walk up Mount Rogers for an afternoon hunt. After walking slowly together for several miles, Dean said to me, "Uncle Dick, you sure sound out of breath and if you got this idea of climbing Kilimanjaro next year, you had better start getting in shape."

That was a wake-up call to me. On the following Monday, the snow started to fall about two inches an hour, and we decided if we were going to get that camper and our gear out of those mountains before spring, we had better start packing. We loaded up and within a few hours were out of the mountains on clear roads back to Abingdon, Virginia, and to Banner Elk, North Carolina. Within the next two days, more than three feet of snow fell in those mountains.

After the next couple of days, the snow had stopped in Banner Elk with a total of about twenty inches on the ground. I told my wife Dede that if I was serious about this idea of climbing Kilimanjaro on my 70th birthday, then I had better start training here and now.

It was almost Thanksgiving 2008, and the snow was deep on Beech Mountain where we live above the vineyards. I started serious training by hiking up Beech Mountain in the snow with my trusty dog friend Coffee. We started up the mountain as shown in the previous photographs on November 21, 2008, and I soon was out of breath. I knew then that I had a lot of work to do to get in shape for Mount Kilimanjaro which was less than fourteen months away.

During the next fourteen months, I have hiked those two and three-mile trails almost daily, thinking that would surely get me in shape for Kilimanjaro. On Christmas 2008, I bought both my sons and Dean a pair of trekking poles and suggested that if they were serious about joining me that they should start hiking as much as they could in the next year. I really don't think any of the three believed that I was serious about Kilimanjaro. I had offered each of them the opportunity to join me, but I was determined to go by myself if no one could join me. After all, this was my *Bucket List* of things to do, not necessarily theirs, and it started with me when I saw that movie, *Snows of Kilimanjaro,* in 1957. How could I expect them to share in that desire other than just being with me?

I developed several different routes around the nearby mountains to give some variety to the morning hike as well as to make those hikes more difficult and more uphill. I live at 4100 feet elevation, and the hikes to Beech Mountain could take me up to 5500 feet and be extended six to eight miles. Coffee, my chocolate Labrador, was always with me, running ahead or chasing deer or turkeys. He finally learned to come back when I blew on a whistle, so I worried less about a local bear, wolf or mountain lion getting him.

In the spring of 2008, I purchased three acres of pasture land on the south slope of Beech Mountain about 1.5 miles above the winery in the valley. We planted a vineyard of grapes consisting of the Seyval Blanc, Cabernet Sauvignon, and Riesling varieties. This was to become the highest vineyard in the eastern United States resting at an elevation of 4900 feet. I recognized at the beginning that planting vineyards in these mountains of North Carolina was indeed challenging, and many thought that I was crazy to plant vineyards at these elevations. But now we have proven, over the past nine years, that this area of North Carolina may become the best area in the USA for growing quality wine grapes of European origin. With vineyards planted on the south slopes above the valley floor like in Europe, we are making wines most similar to those of Europe's High Country. The photograph below is one of the established vineyards on the south slopes of Beech Mountain that I hiked to almost daily in my preparation for climbing Mount Kilimanjaro.

I mention this vineyard location because it gave me a clear reason to hike and climb to that vineyard and an adjacent vineyard almost daily during the year before the climb. The grade was steep, at least as steep as I thought Kilimanjaro might be, though it was proven during the climb to the summit that I underestimated the steepness of Mount Kilimanjaro. As I climbed to that vineyard with Coffee during cold windy weather, I would imagine that I was climbing Kilimanjaro and play games with myself, saying, *This is not too cold or too windy.* Again,

The vineyard on the south slopes of Beech Mountain that I would practice climbing to near the mountain top

I later learned different.

On my 69ᵗʰ birthday on January 11, 2009, as shown in the photograph, I climbed beyond the 1.5 miles to the vineyard and into the town and ski resort of Beech Mountain resting at 5500 feet. I began to take this round trip hike of seven miles at least once every couple of weeks. I would stop for lunch at the Fred's Hardware and Deli, and Coffee and I would hike back to the winery in something less than four hours. Those working at Fred's would always smile and ask if I was still planning to Climb Mount Kilimanjaro. They thought it was a pretty good hike to get to their store from the winery in Banner Elk. But, I knew if I was going to have a chance at reaching the summit of Mount Kilimanjaro one year later, I had better prepare myself as well as I could by climbing these local mountains of North Carolina.

When we had visitors, or my son Travis and his wife Janet would visit, like in October 2009, we made that hike to let them experience the climb and to see how they would fare. Travis and Janet had little difficulty with the climb except that the altitude did have a slight impact upon them, as they live near sea level outside of Charleston, South Carolina.

I felt pretty strong at that point, which was good since it was less

Climbing to Beech Mountain from Banner Elk Winery on
my 69ᵗʰ birthday along with Coffee

*Travis climbed with me and Coffee to the top of the town of
Beech Mountain, North Carolina, on October 6, 2009.*

than three more months until I would actually attempt the climb of
Kilimanjaro. I know that Travis, who is now 39, was very pleased that I
could climb to Beech Mountain as well as he did. He said to me as we
walked back together along the trail, "Dad, I had some doubts that you
were serious about climbing Mount Kilimanjaro, but now, I believe that
you can actually make it to the summit." There was pride in his voice to
see me in pretty good physical shape.

Before starting on all of this hiking and training, in January 2009,
I had my doctor, Dr. Tom Zuber, in Boone, North Carolina, give me a
complete physical exam, including a nuclear stress test. I wanted him
to know that I was thinking about climbing Kilimanjaro and wanted to
find out the best that I could, without an invasive test, just how my heart
was doing. I have long known that I have an irregular or premature heart
beat that shows up on an EKG. So, Dr. Zuber suggested that this test
might be a good indicator of how well my heart pumped under stress.
Dr. Zuber also knew that I was being treated for high blood pressure.
Once the results came back OK, Dr. Zuber explained that my heart
pumped better than the average for my age and he felt my heart would

not prevent me from reaching the summit, that maybe the altitude would be the main concern. He also said that living here in the Banner Elk area at 4100 feet might just become a real advantage in helping me become better acclimated to the high altitude of Kilimanjaro, which is above 19,000 feet.

During 2009, I continued to climb and hike these local mountains daily for an hour or so. My pace became faster and my legs became stronger. In fact, one night in November 2009, now only six weeks before the climb, my wife, ten years younger, said to me, "Darling, it is dark and I can't see your gray hair, but if I didn't know better, by the feel of your body and legs, I would think that I am in bed with a younger man." What a boost to my ego. Nothing she could have said to me would have been more satisfying.

My father died of a heart attack at 67 caused by his black lung disease, and my sister died of a heart attack in 2001, at the age of 55. These facts, and my irregular heart beat, had given me a concern about my heart. However, with Dr. Zuber's exam and my wife's observation, I continued to concentrate on my goal of reaching Mount Kilimanjaro on my 70th Birthday on January 11, 2010.

I did visit my doctor one more time near the end of December, 2009. I called to check on medications for malaria that I'd gotten from the Watauga County Health Department and any interactions with what I was already taking. Dr. Zuber wanted to see me one more time, as he said he wasn't sure I was serious about the climb when he'd examined me in January. After shots to prevent flu and tetanus, he gave me a clean bill of health to proceed. I was off to Africa and Mount Kilimanjaro.

CHAPTER 3

Planning and Booking the Climb

In the summer of 2009, I chatted with visitors to the Banner Elk Winery and Inn about climbing Kilimanjaro. In fact, I tried to encourage several of those folks whom I had gotten to know pretty well to join me on the expedition. Several gave the idea some serious consideration. I hoped that my two sons, Eric and Travis, might join me but they couldn't leave responsibilities at home. I encouraged my nephew Dean Yates and Dean's father, Tom Yates, to go with me. I told Tom that if he didn't want to make the climb attempt, then he could wait for us at the Kilimanjaro Mountain Resort and join us on our planned five-day Safari into the Serengeti.

I purchased the book, *Kilimanjaro—A Trekking Guide to Africa's Highest Mountain,* written by Henry Stedman, and read it carefully every night. Now that I have climbed Kilimanjaro, I feel this book is an accurate source of information and worth reading and studying by anyone interested in climbing Mount Kilimanjaro and the adjacent Mount Meru. My nephew, Dean, also purchased the book and studied it well. In addition, I also rented the movie, *Snows of Kilimanjaro,* and purchased Ernest Hemingway's book of short stories that included the one that inspired the move. It should be pointed out that neither the movie nor the book includes anything about climbing that mountain, but more on the human drama of hunting in the surrounding foothills. Of course, during the climb and return I did see a lot of that environment and the animals that roamed the foothills of Kilimanjaro.

The stories and accounts of those that have climbed Kilimanjaro that are posted on the Internet became my main source of information of what to expect, the type of clothes needed, and the difficulty of the climb. Also, while at the winery, I met two men who had personal information: one doctor who had climbed to the summit, Mr. Eddie Montgomery from Danville, Kentucky; and one professor from the

University of South Carolina. Both of these gentlemen shared with me the difficulty of the climb even more accurately than the books and Internet accounts. But then again, both of these gentlemen are some ten years younger than myself.

They both said that my hikes around the mountains here in Banner Elk were too short and that I should extend those hikes to six to eight miles per day. Now that I have climbed Kilimanjaro, I certainly agree with that suggestion, but it is always a time constraint that we each have to work within and maintain our current jobs. As I look back on my life and career, I realize that I could not have spared the time from existing jobs and night school studies to have even considered training or climbing that mountain until this particular time in my life.

As the winter of 2009 turned into spring and into summer, it became obvious that my friends who had considered the idea, as well as my two sons, were having difficulty finding the time to train or consider going with me. In the fall, my nephew DeanYeats started to give some serious consideration to the idea, but he still had a lot to work out in addition to starting to train on those mountains near where he lived in Abingdon, Virginia. I knew that Dean had the best chance of going with me, but he has three small children, and his wife and father were not too keen on the idea of him taking off to Africa with me. I made it clear to my sons, and to Dean, that I was not putting any pressure on them and that I understood the difficulty each faced. No doubt, all three love me and did not want me to go by myself, but I let them know I was going no matter what, even if I had to go by myself.

I think they finally realized, about October, that I was serious. When Travis visited with me on October 6, 2009, we scaled the steepest slopes of Beech Mountain with him huffing and puffing alongside me. As we walked backed down from the town of Beech Mountain that beautiful October day, as shown in the photograph, Travis said to me, "Dad, I wish more than anything that I could go with you, but for me to take two weeks away from my job, I know that I would be fired, and I need this job during these most difficult economic situations."

I told him that I understood, and at his age of 39, I would not have been able to go even with my own father. I knew it was not Travis' goal, but he would only go to be with me. I also told him, but in reality showed him, that I was ready to make that attempt to climb that mountain in Africa, for it had been my own personal goal for almost 53 years.

Travis and me walking back from the hike to
Beech Mountain on October 6, 2009

In October, I made tentative arrangements with the African Walking Company. They provided a good summary of what was needed and what it would cost. Also, I looked at the various travel schedules with airlines and the cost. I had told both my sons and Dean that I would cover all costs for any of them to go, but we had to finalize our bookings by mid-November.

Dean told me during our annual hunting and fishing trip that he was going to join me and that he had it all worked out with his family, his dad, and his father-in-law. Dean has a landscaping business in Abingdon and expected that business would be rather slow during January. Travis and Eric could not go. So, I booked the deal for Dean and me with the airlines to leave on January 8, 2009, from Charlotte, North Carolina, Via Amsterdam and then on KLM to Mt. Kilimanjaro International Airport.

My brother-in-law, Tom Yates, Dean's father, invited my wife and me to join him and his family for our annual Thanksgiving dinner together at his house in Abingdon. There must have been forty people from various sides of the families. That is when Tom told me that I should talk with Dean's wife Angie to help her feel more comfortable about Dean going. That is when I realized that Dean did not have all his approvals, and even his father-in-law had some reservations about his son-in-law leaving his family and his business all in the hands of his daughter Angie in the dead of winter.

Before talking with Angie, I took Dean aside and said, "Dean, are you sure you can make this trip to Africa?"

Dean said, "Uncle Dick, I have it covered, and I am not letting you go by yourself."

I spoke with Angie, and she just smiled and listened without saying much as I explained that I will be looking after him, and that this trip will be a life-changing experience for Dean. I also predicted that he would want to take her and the kids back to Africa sometime in the future. I tried to focus more on the safari than the climb, but that did not seem to help. Angie just gave me that lovely smile and showed me her warm understanding and love for Dean. By the time Thanksgiving dinner was over and all the doubting Thomases had spoken to me, the trip was on, and Dean was ready to start working out and training in earnest.

During the winter days of December, Dean would call me from some high mountain peaks around Abingdon, Virginia, and say "Uncle Dick, I have this fifteen-pound pack on my back and walked about five miles, but I am so tired, that I don't know if I can make it back home."

I said, "Keep walking and pretend that you are on Mount Kilimanjaro." I too began to carry a backpack, and it made my daily hikes even tougher. I realized that I should have been carrying a backpack with water—not for the past month but for the past year. It was clear that my back was not as strong as it was when I was younger.

Dean left all the arrangements to me: to select the route, the plane schedule and the booking arrangements with the African Walking Company. He said, "Uncle Dick, just tell me when we are to leave and how much weight I can pack in my duffle bag and in my backpack, and I will be there."

So, the flight out of Charlotte on January 8, 2010, was set. We would spend my birthday on the first night of the climb which would be on January 11, 2010.

During my research on the Internet, talking with the African Walking Company contact in London and by reading the book, *Kilimanjaro*, I discovered five possible routes to the summit: the Shira Route; the Machame Route; the Umbawe Route; the Marangu Route; and the

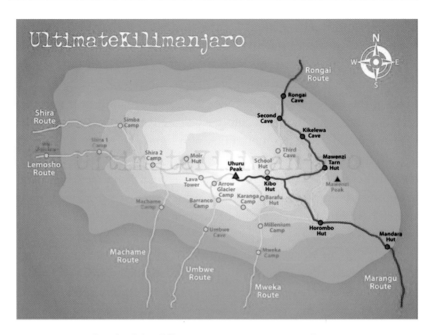

Sketch of the different mountain routes to the summit
with the Rongai Route highlighted

Northern Rongai Route starting near Kenya. I selected the Rongai Route. These different routes as shown in the mountain sketch above were taken from the Ulitimate Kilimanjaro website on the Internet.

The reason for selecting the Rongai route had as much to do with our schedule as anything. Dean and I both wanted to go on a safari into the Serengeti after the climb. The Rongai route is a six-day schedule with four days to get to the base camp at Kibo Hut and on the fifth day, starting midnight to reach the summit. This route from the base camp at Kibo Hut would take us first to the crater's edge at Gilman's Point while passing the famous Hans Meyer Cave where Mr. Meyer stayed overnight on his famous climb to the summit in 1889. Then the summit is reached by hiking the crater's edge to Stella's Point, and then to the summit at Uhuru Peak.

The Rongai route is the only route that approaches Mount Kilimanjaro from the north, close to the Kenyan border. This route, although gaining in popularity among climbers, still experiences low traffic. The Rongai is the preferred route for those looking for an alternative to the easier and more crowded Marangu route. The Marangu route is sometimes called the *Coca Cola®* route because the path to the

Kibo Hut and the base camp for the summit is well graded and they have huts with beds to stay in rather than tents.

Because Dean and I are both light sleepers, I could not imagine sleeping in a hut with twenty other people snoring or getting up at all times of the night to go to the toilet. Dean and I had experienced that type of scenario many times before when we went hunting and fishing with our buddies in the mountains of Virginia. Dean and I quickly agreed that the Rongai route was our route even though that route is more difficult due to climbing over volcanic rocks, and there is less time to become acclimated to the altitude. We felt that we would hike higher at each base camp to help with acclimation and that is exactly what we did at each campsite.

Although the scenery is not as varied as in the western routes, Rongai makes up for this by passing through true wilderness areas for days where wildlife roams, including elephants and Cape Buffalo. In addition, on our descent from the mountain, we returned by a different route, the Marangu route. That gave us a more varied view of the mountain than returning down the same path that was taken on the climb upward. True enough, we did see droppings of elephants and Cape Buffalo but did not actually see them, although on the second night at the Kikelewa Cave Campsite, I did feel and hear a large animal of sorts stumble over our tent rope. It just about pulled the tent down, waking me up with a loud shout and I shouted to it to "Get Out Of Here!"

All then settled down, and I went back to sleep.

On our return from the summit down the Marangu route we stopped for our box lunch. I took a quick look inside the wooden huts with beds, and they appeared quite comfortable. It was mentioned that when President Carter climbed and reached the summit of Kilimanjaro in August, 1988, at the age of 64, he took the Marangu route, no doubt for security reasons so his group could all stay together. Both of these two routes—the Marangu and the Rongai route—they both lead to Kibo Hut then follow the same path upwards to the summit at Uhuru Peak via Gilman's point and Stella's Point. Kilimanjaro saves its most grueling trail for the last leg of the journey.

In making our arrangements for travel to Kilimanjaro, I took into account that the weather could be bad here in the states during early January and had intentionally scheduled a layover day at the Kilimanjaro Mountain Resort. That way, we could get adjusted to the difference in the time change while also giving us a little extra time if the planes scheduled got delayed because of bad weather. As it turned out, a snow storm was forming in the midwest on January 6, so I contacted Delta is see if we could fly from Charlotte to Atlanta rather than going from Charlotte to Detroit and then to Amsterdam. Changing the flight would mean a massive increase in cost, plus the Delta contact said that Detroit Airport could handle the snow better than the fog expected in Atlanta. I knew if we missed the scheduled Delta flight to Amsterdam, we could miss the start of our climb on Monday morning, January 11.

The Delta contact suggested that we go to Charlotte and catch the 9:30 a.m. flight to Detroit, rather than take the original flight scheduled for 12:30 p.m. We made that change, but it also meant that we had to leave Boone, North Carolina, on Thursday evening, January 7, and spend an extra night near the Charlotte Douglas Airport. We left Boone that evening already in the snow as shown in the photograph below and arrived in Charlotte, some three hours later. We had a nice dinner and then watched the national football championship between Alabama and Texas, and as we all know, Alabama won the National Championship.

Leaving Boone on January 7, 2010, Dean in his "Chinese looking hat" that he planned to wear to the summit and me in my "Indiana Jones" hat to give me some extra confidence in just starting out on this adventure

We both looked a little funny dressed as we were with backpacks and hats walking around the airports in Detroit and Amsterdam. Several people asked where we were going and we said with pride, "To climb Mount Kilimanjaro in Africa." They then looked at my gray hair and walked away shaking their heads with a smile of doubt.

There was plenty of snow when we arrived in the morning at the Amsterdam airport. With about five hours to wait for the KLM airplane to Kilimanjaro International Airport, we slept a little on a bench and I bought a can of "florigra" (*foie gras*) for Dean to try. I knew this was a new taste for Dean, and it was well worth the $20 as Dean got his first taste of this French delicacy.

Catching that earlier flight from Charlotte on January eighth was a great move, for it got us into Detroit with plenty of time, about six hours, to catch the 4 p.m. flight to Amsterdam. As it turned out, the 12:30 p.m. flight from Charlotte was delayed and did not arrive in Detroit in time to have made the connection to Amsterdam. So our first decision to go earlier and wait in the Detroit airport was the correct one.

Snow was falling when we arrived in Amsterdam and our warm clothes felt good. The KLM flight was on time leaving at 11 a.m. to arrive that Saturday evening in Kilimanjaro at 9:30 p.m. The trip to Kilimanjaro, Tanzania, was an adventure in itself as it involved four flights from Charlotte, North Carolina. Almost three hours to Detroit, then eight hours to Amsterdam, five hours wait, and then another nine hours to Kilimanjaro, which is the passage most westerners are routed on the way to the Kilimanjaro International Airport. Dean and I decided not to fly to Nairobi even though it is cheaper, because one needs a visa for entering Kenya, and you can buy a visa for Tanzania at the airport for about $100 dollars. Our flight arrived on time at around 9:30 p.m. local time, a journey of 29 hours from when we left Charlotte.

On arriving in Kilimanjaro, at a temperature of about 85°F. we immediately waited in line along with about three hundred others to obtain our visa. They had several lines for the visa and we obtained ours within an hour and then proceeded through customs. No doubt, Tanzania is doing well on the visa income which amounts to about $30,000 per plane from outside the country.

On retrieving our luggage and finding it all in good shape, we proceeded outside where a driver was waiting with our names on a poster sign to drive us the hour or so ride to the Kilimanjaro Mountain

Resort. This was our first exposure to the night life between the airport and the resort. A few miles beyond the airport, we were stopped by a police road block. The driver said to us, "No problem, just a normal check." Apparently, the sign on our Land Rover saying Mt. Kilimanjaro Mountain Resort cleared the way for us to proceed onward.

It was night, about midnight, and we saw little except some bar signs and the lights of Arsuha. We soon turned off the paved road onto a rough dirt road winding through what looked like little huts and banana trees. My first thought was that this resort is out in the boondocks. We soon passed the Kili Hotel where the driver pointed out that was where President Carter stayed in 1988, getting ready for his climb. Within fifteen minutes, we arrived at the iron gate leading into the very luxurious Mt. Kilimanjaro Mountain Resort. Everyone was expecting us, and a clean twin bed was all I needed to be happy. This hotel is gated and has such amenities as a gift shop, pool, massage services and the Internet as well as their own rooster to wake us up at daylight.

That rooster would not shut up. I told Dean that rooster was the first thing I wanted to find after breakfast, because I knew he must have been just outside our window, and he would be there tomorrow morning as well.

Our first day in Africa was a recovery day from jetlag and the rooster. We had a nice breakfast by the pool and then decided to take a hike around the nearby village with a guide who was waiting for customers outside the hotel. The guide worked for tips.

We toured the local village and nearby waterfalls. The waterfall was in a steep mountain ravine and about four miles away. But to walk eight miles is nothing for those of the Chang tribe who lived near the resort for that is their main method of travel. It took about five hours to complete the tour, and it was indeed an eye opener. A little boy showed us his toy and skill of running a plastic lid from a 5-gallon bucket guided by a wooden stick.

What was most interesting to me was that I learned that same skill with a similar lid when I was a small boy of his age in West Virginia. We gave this little boy a dollar bill tip and he was thrilled as you can see in the photograph. So were the ladies we met on their way to church and offered them a dollar each to allow us to take our picture with them. The one lady after the photo said laughingly while still holding the dollar bill, "Do you want a repeat?"

Our tour continued through the banana and avocado trees until we climbed down a steep hill to the valley floor of the waterfall as shown in the next photograph. These photographs show just how friendly the local people were to us and what we were to expect during the next ten days in Tanzania. This is exactly the type of experience that Dean and I were seeking and this first day was truly a delightful experience.

The little boy playing with his toy and the ladies in their colorful outfits on their way to church in the nearby village of the Kilimanjaro Mountain Resort

The waterfalls near the Kilimanjaro Mountain Resort

At six o'clock that Sunday evening, the climbers assembled for a briefing by the African Walking Company. The briefing was conducted by an expert guide named Amani who had climbed to the summit about thirty-five times during the past years. Amani had been the chief guide when President Carter climbed Mount Kilimanjaro in 1988. He spoke excellent English and he handed out any gear that we had ordered from home. For example, I had rented a down sleeping bag and pad, a down jacket, and two trekking poles. Several others in our group did the same thing but a few including Dean had brought their own jackets, poles, pads and sleeping bags.

Amani said very clearly that there were three Golden Rules for climbing to the summit of Mount Kilimanjaro: first, go slowly, slowly or polee, polee in Swahili which allows one to become better acclimated and to not over exert oneself; secondly, have a positive attitude about your own ability to make the climb; thirdly, drink plenty of water for that helps in oxygenation of your body. Amani also said the African Walking Company always suggests to the various guides on the climb to take all who want to climb another 1000 feet higher after arriving at the campsite to help in the acclimation.

We then got to meet the other ten members of our group and all had an excellent dinner in the main dining room of the resort. We found out that we had five from the United Kingdom, one from Spain, one from Russia who was now married to a man from the States who was with us, two from Australia and Dean and myself making up the full dozen. We all seemed to click together, sharing each other's desire and some of our experiences. I soon learned that I was the only gray haired guy in the group and some 45 years older than the youngest girl from the UK and seventeen years older than the second-eldest man who was a doctor from Australia. This doctor, named Michael Hoopman, was making the climb with his daughter, Savannah, who was in her final year of studying medicine. We all were certain to get to know each other better in the coming days.

CHAPTER 4

Tanzania
Mount Kilimanjaro Resort Villagers

Dean and I knew when we left on this African expedition that this trip was going to be a life-changing experience for both of us. Little did we know what was ahead of us or who we would meet that would have such an impact. The most eye opening observation to me occurred once we arrived in Tanzania and traveled through the small villages and towns near Mount Kilimanjaro. Something was obvious to me—the similarity of life in Tanzania to what my own life had been sixty and seventy years ago in and around the small coal mining town of Sophia, West Virginia. For example, when I was a small boy, we walked everywhere we went. We dressed up in our best on Sunday and walked to church. As Dean and I walked around the village near the Mount Kilimanjaro Resort, we saw hundreds of people, dressed up in their finest, walking to church.

The villagers walking to church in their finest clothes

Dean cutting grass with a sickle while the
Tanzanians watched and laughed

I remember so well, Mom hanging our newly washed clothes on an outside line to dry. That same technique of drying clothes is the standard now in these nearby villages around Mount Kilimanjaro. We saw families washing their clothes on rocks near the creeks and taking baths. I did that also when I was young. Most of the roads were dirt roads and were maintained mostly by hand. All the grass was cut by hand with a sickle. Dean, as shown in the above photograph, even tried his hand at cutting grass but I had enough of that exercise when I was a young boy.

We toured one particular village where the locals had just butchered a goat as shown in the following photograph. This was nothing new to Dean and me for we had butchered many a deer during our hunting experience. However, what I knew that Dean had only heard about, is when I was a young boy, one of my jobs at home was raising a hog. Then in the fall, I had to watch my dad and Uncle Foggie kill and butcher that hog for our winter meat. My job then, along with my cousins and neighbor boys, was gathering the wood to build the fire hot enough to boil the water needed to scald the hog to remove the hair. As a reward, we were then given the bladder to clean out and insert a hollow stick into so we could blow it up to make a ball that we could bounce and play with. While these boys did not run along with a bladder ball, these villagers wasted nothing, and used every part of the goat for some form.

The butchered goat

These simple observations of the similarity of my young life with those now in the rural areas of Tanzania hit a soft spot in my heart that I could relate to. For Dean, this was all a new experience and one that he had never before seen, as is true of so many people today. For me it was like stepping back in time.

As I got to know my guide, Atilio, while we climbed Mount Kilimanjaro together, he could not believe my early life had been much like his own. I believe he had the image that all Americans have wealthy families and live in big houses most of their life. As Atilio got to know me, I believe he realized that I, like most Americans, never had a silver spoon in my mouth and achieved improvements through both hard work and good education. I feel sure Atilio will look at Americans now in a different light since he and the others have met both Dean and me.

Atilio and his wife have twin children, one boy and one girl, who are now six years old. Atilio has taken his income from guiding on Mount Kilimanjaro to send them both to private schools. This way they learn the English language first, before Swahili, so that better future opportunities will be available to them to attend high schools with better educational programs. Atilio and his wife cultivate a small piece of land of about three acres to raise corn and other vegetables that they can barter with the school to supplement any additional cash cost needed for their children's tuition.

Atilio has now become one of the key guides for the African Walking Company and is available to become a personal guide to anyone interested in climbing Mount Kilimanjaro.

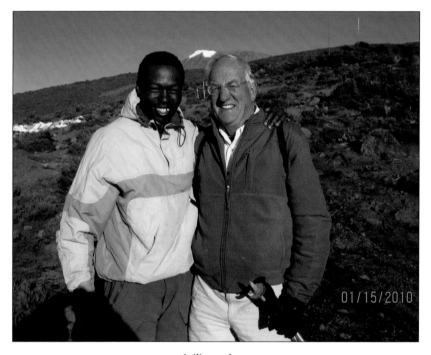

Atilio and me

CHAPTER 5

The Climb to Mount Kilimanjaro

Day 1: January 11, 2010
Rongai Route Trailhead
at 6600 feet elevation and 90°F.

The day had finally come—hard to believe, but true. Kilimanjaro towered nearly 16,000 feet above the hotel, its summit hidden by clouds.

We all arrived for breakfast at the same time, which seemed remarkable, and all were excited to finally get on the trail and start climbing. We had a nice breakfast at the hotel and then checked in our stuff that we would be leaving at the hotel in storage until we returned in six days. We piled our packs and duffels into and on top of two Land Rover vans and started out.

The Rongai route is not very popular because of the nearly three-hour drive to the trailhead. But what an experience! You drive through the various towns and villages and see how the people work and live, which to me was one of the most pleasant experiences. I would say that 90% of the folks in Tanzania do not have cars or bikes, so they're all on the roads walking about their business. You see women carrying bananas on their heads, carrying water, chickens, and all sorts of food on their heads while some men are running down the streets with carts full of produce going to the market. There was an occasional car or van but they were usually ferrying tourists around. Our driver did a great job weaving around the heavy activity on the roads and it was pure entertainment, but at times I feared we could have a wreck even before we got to the trailhead.

The drivers were impressive, handling the Land Rovers through mud and dirt roads when there was no pavement. We were in the van with the senior climbing guide, named Toshi Minja, who wanted to take the lead from the van that started out before us. Our driver took a short cut through a muddy road, coming out ahead of the other van by a mere six feet. I do believe he could become a NASCAR driver.

We checked in at the gate and had our box lunch while the second group of twelve arrived, making the total of 24 in the two groups arranged by the African Walking Company. The various porters of about three per climber amounted to a total of 36 as our support team, including six professional guides who would take us to the summit in the next five days. The various selected porters divvied up their loads. The limit for each porter is supposedly 35 pounds, but with all the tents, poles, food and other supplies, it appeared to me that each porter was carrying more either on his head and back or in his hands.

We finally started the climb about 1 p.m. I checked my thermometer, and it was 89 degrees as we started up through the rainforest. It soon started raining. We quickly covered our packs and continued to walk through the various corn and potato fields for the first half of the hike. The agricultural land soon gave way to an alpine forest. We passed a few villagers, and some of the kids were carrying wood sticks as shown in the first photograph. Dean and I passed out candy and coins and the word spread fast as to who in the climbing group to follow. For a while Dean was the Pied Piper.

We saw our first colobus monkeys about a mile up the trail as three or four of them were sitting on stumps and active in the trees near the edge of the fields. The pace was very slow, which was expected but hard to adjust to as it was a third of the pace I had trained for back in the mountains of North Carolina. I soon had a mind adjustment saying to myself, *Why am I in a hurry? This is what I came for and there is no place to go except to our first campsite, so enjoy the slower pace and relax.* That is what I did for the rest of the climb.

We walked through the rain and pine forest, climbing steadily for a total of about four hours, until we emerged from the forest and into the next climate zone, the moorlands. We soon arrived at our first campsite at the Moorland Bivouac. Our tents were set up, and a hot cup of tea awaited, along with some popcorn as a snack. We found our tent and duffle bags and then took another climb, along with a guide, for about an hour to a higher altitude and returned to camp for dinner. The temperature was now in the 70's with misty clouds.

First campsite at the Moorland Bivouac at 2600 meters (8,528 ft)

Tent arrangements for two people along with sleeping bags and mats.
(The tents were located on as flat a surface as possible with only a few rocks.)

After the afternoon acclimation climb of about 1000 feet, we returned to our camp for a lovely evening meal. Before each meal, the porter would bring us a pan of hot water and say, "Time to washie, washie." This became one of our group's phrases as it may relate to any situation that occurred. We were all surprised at the quality of our first evening meal, which consisted of hot celery and bean soup, fried chicken and mashed potatoes and other vegetables. The only thing that I missed was the gravy which I recognize is only a Southern boy's delicacy.

After dinner, Dean spoke up and said he had a surprise. That is when the six guides and the cook brought in a birthday cake with the big 70 candle on top singing, "Happy Birthday to Babu Wolfe." Other than Dean, I do not believe anyone else in the group knew it was my birthday and that I was 70.

The nickname of "Babu," which means Grandfather in Swahili, is a lovely gift from one of the guides called Atilio. I had talked with Atilio during our initial hike and we liked each other from the start. Atilio would later become my most trusted and dearest African friend who was instrumental in **my** making the summit some four days later.

The 70th birthday cake with the Chief Guide Toshi on the right and the Assistant Guide Atilio, in his Massai robe, who gave me the nickname of "Babu" meaning Grandfather Wolfe. The chief cook in the white hat made the cake.

No doubt, Dean had made all the arrangements ahead of time so the cake could be baked in the field tent which must have not been an easy task.

Dean and I celebrated my 70th birthday with cake.
What a precious moment for me!

Dean knew what he was planning for my birthday even before he left the States. He just didn't know how he would achieve it all but knew that he would make it happen somehow. That is just the kind of confidence and "going outside the box" that makes Dean such a successful person in whatever he does.

We have slept in tents together before while hunting, and I knew Dean did not snore, so we both slept well, except for my needing to get up several times during the night to go to the toilet. I was not going outside the tent, for I was not sure what was out there, so I solved my problem with a zip lock bag. Dean finally caught on the next night as well.

There was an outside toilet made within a small rectangular tent with a five-gallon bucket and a toilet seat. This became a darling arrangement for all twelve of us throughout our climb and was preferable to some of the fixed toilets at a couple of the sites. These consisted of a hole in the floor with a nearby broom. I mention this toilet arrangement for those who read this book so you know what to expect. This climb is about as rough as it can get for the toilet arrangements but has been practiced by humans for eons. So, if you expect to make this climb to the "Roof of Africa," the fourth highest mountain in the world, then you must get toughened up. This climb is certainly no Sunday cake walk or a drive in the country with nearby modern toilet facilities.

The next morning when we got out of our tents and the fog had cleared partially for a little while, we got our first glimpse of Mount Kilimanjaro some twenty miles away.

First view of Mount Kilimanjaro some twenty miles away from Campsite No. 1 at the Moorland Bivouac on the morning of January 12, 2010

Day 2: January 12, 2010
Moorland Bivouac Camp No. 1 at 2600 Meters
(8,518 feet) to Campsite No. 2 at Kikelewa Caves
Bivouac at 3600 meters (11,808 feet)

The early morning climb up across the moorland and heather gave a good view of Kilimanjaro which excited all of us even though we knew it was still twenty miles away. We were now climbing over volcanic rocks and boulders scattered about some million years ago from the eruption of Kilimanjaro. We were now heading towards our second base camp at the Kikelewa Caves Bivouac some eight miles away and 3800 foot gain in altitude. This campsite is located at 3600 meters (11,808 feet).

This day was no doubt the toughest day of the trek, other than the climb to the summit. What made it so difficult was the climbing up and over the rocks. It was important to know where to place your feet to not twist an ankle or pull a muscle. However, the eight hours of climbing was complemented by the beautiful scenery and the flowers were unbelievably bright and colorful. Dean, being a horticulture specialist and having his own nursery, really enjoyed the flora and its colors as well as knowing most of the plants by name.

Climbing over volcanic rocks on the eight-hour trek to our second campsite

Dean looking back at the plateau from which we started
the climb less than two days ago

Nearing the second campsite, Dean took a long view of where we had just climbed as he looked back at the plateau below where we had started less than two days ago. This is the most rugged part of the climb and one of the most exhausting days for me.

During this second day's climb, both Dean and I got to know several of the guides as we climbed along with them. This was when we first came to know Atilio Hemedi, who shared his experiences on climbing this mountain, first as a porter for four years and now a guide for the past two years. Atilio spoke English so well, was so helpful and friendly with such a great smile and personally, that we established an immediate friendship bond. Atilio was 31 and had twin children, one girl and one boy of six years old. He showed us pictures, and Dean in turn showed pictures of his three children. Atilio was from the Pare Tribe who are one of the largest tribes around Kilimanjaro. In fact, it is the Pare Tribe members who spent generations climbing and establishing villages around this mountain. One characteristic of the Pare Tribe is that they are short people with strong climbing legs and backs. Atilio also had some relationship through his father with the Maasai Tribe because he would sometimes put around his shoulders a beautiful and colorful Maasai robe called a "Shuka."

We both learned so much from Atilio about life on this mountain.

In fact, he told us that the people who die most often on the mountain are not the climbers, but the young porters. Many of these porters need a job and are not strong enough to carry the large loads or do not have the proper clothing that can withstand this type of terrain and weather.

I asked Atilio what he wanted to do in the future and what he wanted for his children. He said that he wants to become a chief guide and have some of his own clients in a few years. It will take him several more years to earn all the proper certificates, but he is working on that objective. Atilio also said that he wants to give his children a good education so they will not have to earn their living on this mountain. He is now working hard to earn enough money to send them to private schools where they will learn English first in the elementary grades rather than Swahili.

As I talked more with Atilio, he asked me about my own life and if I had an easy life growing because of a rich father. I told him that my dad had been a coal miner in West Virginia and that I grew up much like his kids with not much opportunity. I also told him that my dad had told me much of what he has told his children. My dad would say to me, "Son, get you a good education and that is your ticket out of these coal fields."

My dad, I told Atilio, was much like you in that he did not want me to be a coal miner like himself. "So you see, Atilio, that is exactly what you want for your children, a better life than climbing this mountain."

As we neared the Kikelewa Cave Campsite, Atilio sensed that I was having a little difficulty carrying my backpack of some ten pounds and suggested that he carry it. I felt a little embarrassed by that observation, but also being honest with myself, I said, "Maybe tomorrow you can help me a little and I will carry my own water containers."

When we reached camp, we unloaded, had some tea and soon started out for another climb upwards of maybe 800-1000 feet just for acclimation. All twelve of our group took the climb. The following photographs show the location of CampSite No. 2 at the Kikelewa Caves. Here, during the night, I felt and heard some animal stumble over our tent's anchor rope and just about pull the tent down. I looked outside the next morning for foot prints, but it was too rocky to make out anything. We all ate well that night in the tent, as well as sharing a lot of jokes and good laughs, forming friendships that will last a lifetime. We were getting to know each other and gain admiration for each of our careers and talents.

Dean was getting to know all the guides well and most of the porters.

Campsite No. 2 at the Kikelewa Caves at an elevation of nearly 11,808 feet with the temperature dropping into the 40's

His friendly personality made him the star of our group to all he met. Dean disappeared for a while before dinner that evening, and when he came into the mess tent at 6 p.m., he had a new hair style. He had talked the cook into plaiting his hair as shown in the following photograph. When Atilio saw this new hair style, he immediately started calling Dean "Mzungukichaa," which means in Swahili, "Crazy White Man." All the climbing team started kidding Dean at dinner. I wasn't even sure that I wanted to share the tent with him, but I had seen him do similar things during our annual hunting trips, so I was not surprised.

He took his new nickname with pride and soon all the guides and porters were calling him, "Mzungukichaa" with smiles on their faces.

Dean's new hair style by the cook. Now he was called "Mzungukichaa" for "Crazy White Man."

Day 3: January 13, 2010
Climbing to Mawenzi Tarn Campsite
at 4330 meters (14,200 feet)

This was our day to climb to Mawenzi Tarn Campsite located at the base of the Mawenzi Mountain at an elevation of 4330 meters (14,200 feet.) This was a shorter climb than the previous day but steeper. This day gave everyone a true feeling of the remoteness which is the true beauty of the Rongai Route. The vegetation was soon left behind and the immensity of the mountain loomed like some moon landscape.

The campsite is spectacularly situated in a sheltered cirque directly beneath the towering spires of Mawenzi. This was excellent terrain for the famous giant senecios to grow into impressive specimens.

After arriving at camp, we again took off as a group to climb some higher elevation of the mountain for the sole purpose of seeing the view and becoming better acclimated. We were now starting to function as a team with the hopes that all twelve could reach the summit of Mount Kilimanjaro. In fact, we were behaving like a team, looking after each other, spending time climbing together, and getting to know each other better. We had become a close knit group without consciously trying, because we all realized that we were in this together—maybe for different purposes, but we were like an army unit formed to achieve an important mission.

The photograph on the next page shows the camp as we approached from the south, sitting serenely beneath the mountain edges of the giant sleeping Mawenze Volcano.

The small lake was where we obtained water to drink after boiling. Dean and I always place a purification pill in our drinking water as a precaution. But some of the group did not take this extra precaution, and they had no problems at all.

We arrived at this camp after about five hours of climbing, so we had time to do a little additional climbing for acclimation purposes and to sightsee the surrounding areas.

The group of twelve individuals was really starting to enjoy each other and our guides were enjoying being with us, as shown in the following photograph. The guides encouraged us to climb higher than usual, about another 1500 feet, so that we could see a special view, but also to become better acclimated. They knew the challenge that lay

Dean taking a photograph on our approach to Campsite
No. 3 at Mawenze Tarn at 14,200 feet

Our group of twelve and four guides climbing another 1500 feet to the
rim of one of the Mawenze craters. It is obvious that we are all enjoying
each other and functioning as a team. Maybe we should refer to
ourselves as the "Happy Dozen"

ahead, for the following was the summit day.

The guide, Atilio, is shown giving us a *high five* sign that he was pleased with all of our performances. In fact, he commented that of all the climbs he has made, he has never before seen a group work so well together. He said to me, "Babu, I believe you each have a chance to make it to the top of Kilimanjaro if we keep performing as a team." After returning to base camp, upon Atilio's encouragement, Dean and I still had enough energy and time to climb higher to another special rim of Mawenze so that we could see the different rock monuments made by previous climbers. We added our own contribution to that special art form as shown in the photograph below.

We had a lovely dinner and went to bed early. Dean was enjoying the porters and guides calling him by his new nickname, "Mzungukichaa."

The next morning we heard Atilio bringing a pan of hot water and saying, "Washie, washie," to the people in the tent next to us.

Dean said to me, "Watch this." As Atilio was placing the pan of hot water at the front of our tent and starting to say, "Washie, washie," Dean rapidly unzipped the front of the tent, stuck his head out saying loudly, "Mzungukichaa!"

Atilio fell backwards with fright, spilling the hot water, and with his feet in the air. They both began to laugh as other guides watched in amazement. The bond of friendship had been established between us and Atilio.

Dean and me at the special rock art formations left by previous climbers on the rim high about the Mawenze Tarn Campsite No. 3 at nearly 15,200 feet

Day 4: January 14, 2010
Five hour climb from Mawenzi Camp to the Base Camp of Kilimanjaro called "Kibo Hut" at 4700 meters (15, 416 feet)

Today, we began our five-hour hike up and over the foothills of Mawenze into what is called "The Saddle," resting between the two volcanoes of Mawenzi and the towering Mount Kilimanjaro. My friendship with Atilio had continued to grow. Before leaving camp after breakfast, Atilio wrapped me in his Maasai Shuka and wished me God's speed and strength as shown in the following photograph. I can't begin to tell you how touching and meaningful that small private ceremony was to me. I know now, Atilio knew better than I what difficulties and challenges lay ahead.

Atilio wrapping me "Babu" in his Maasai Shuka as a blessing of friendship and strength in preparation for the summit climb

Atilio suggested, now as my coach, that I should drink as much water as possible and eat as much as I could to gather energy in preparation for the summit attempt very early the next morning. To make sure that I did drink a lot of water, even before starting the climb across *The Saddle*, Atilio and I toasted each other by each drinking a half-liter of water out of my two water bottles with a Banner Elk Winery label. See the following photograph with Mount Kilimanjaro looming in the background.

Atilio and me toasting each other with a drink of water from my two water bottles carrying the Banner Elk Winery label (After the climb, I gave these two bottles with labels to Atilio to give to his two children.)

At this point in the climb, Dean and I had shown no effect of Acute Mountain Sickness (AMS), but some of the others in the group were now experiencing headaches, slight dizziness, loss of appetite and nausea.

The expansive saddle area reminded me of pictures of the lunar landscape. The wind was blowing steadily, but was not a serious problem. The expansive view of this area made me feel like the early settlers might have felt as they crossed some of the USA western deserts on their way to California. There weren't a lot of places to rest along the trail or use the toilet in this Alpine Desert, but Dean did find a way to take a small breather as shown in the following photograph.

Midway across the *Saddle*, we had our box lunch among a cluster of rocks that provided some shelter from the wind. A huge flock of crows joined us looking for leftovers. Nearby were parts of a small plane that had crashed several months earlier killing four people as they tried to find their way across this mountain floor and apparently got into ice that brought the plane down. We all walked slowly by this wreckage which was a reality wake-up call of the magnitude and the seriousness of this elevation and what we were all trying to achieve.

Dean taking a small breather after our box lunch in the middle of the Saddle leading to the base camp (Kibo Hut) with Mount Kilimanjaro looming some eight miles away

Day 5: January 14, 2010
Kibo Hut – The base camp for climbing Kilimanjaro which is located at 4700 meters (15,400 feet)

After walking and climbing another four hours steadily, we finally arrived at Kibo Hut area at 4700 meters (15,400 feet), in the early afternoon. Dean and I were enjoying this moment with Atilio who was just as happy for us, as we arrived in good spirits and ready to start preparation of our gear for the summit starting at midnight. Atilio wanted us to take a picture together in front of the famous Kibo sign pointing out that the first point on the crater rim of Kilimanjaro at Gilman's Point was only five hours away. What we would soon learn is that this is no ordinary five-hour climb. It is the most difficult climb I would ever face.

After arriving at Kibo Hut, Atilio wanted to show Dean and me that we were only five hours away from the first crater rim site on Mount Kilimanjaro. We all looked and felt we were in pretty good shape even though I had an uncertain smile on my face.

We all assembled at the mess tent about 5 p.m. after each of us had finalized our preparations in our own way. It was a much quieter moment among all of us than we had experienced in the past five days. Even Dean was having some time to himself as he slowly and deliberately packed and repacked his backpack with what he thought he might need on the summit attempt.

I started going over my own list, including an extra pair of glasses, head light and batteries, camera, boot laces, bandages, glove and shoe liners, head gear and ear muffs. I sorted out several layers of polyester sweaters and pants, including my lightweight ski pants and my Banner Elk t-shirt that I expected to wear up the mountain. I had climbed enough in extremely cold weather in and around Banner Elk, that I knew about what to wear without getting too hot on the climb upwards.

I placed chocolate M&M candies and nuts in small zipper-lock bags in various jacket pockets so that I could find them for energy. I refilled each water bottle and my camelback carrying two liters of water. I checked the hose that I would drink from, for I knew it was cold enough to freeze the water even now at Kibo Hut. We had to prepare carefully while enough daylight remained to see, for when it gets dark on this mountain, it is difficult to see anything except for the brightest stars that you have even seen.

I have never been in the military service, but I began to imagine what soldiers might feel in some small way when they knew that a battle was pending the very next morning.

When I reflect back now on the total experience gained from this climb and all its months of preparations and anticipations, it has given me a much deeper appreciation of what others have gone through, such as our athletes before the Olympic Games, or a big football game, or our soldiers preparing for battle, or anyone else who is about to face a most challenging situation. These are indeed life-changing experiences and can only be learned through facing these difficult challenges alone.

After an excellent dinner with plenty of carbohydrate foods, hot soups and tea, our chief guide, Tosha, and his assistants came into the tent to explain what to expect the next day. He said that we would be awakened at 11 p.m. so that we could start the climb at midnight. Tosha indicated that he would be leading the group and setting the pace to the summit. Tosha had, during the previous climbs, allowed his assistants to lead and set the pace. Now, the most difficult part of the climb would be his responsibility. He looked each of us over carefully, asked a number of questions, then said, "Goodnight and try to get some sleep because you each are going to need all that you have tomorrow."

I felt in his voice that he knew more than we did of what to expect.

I was ready to jump in the warm mummy sleeping bag along with my polyester sweater, pants and toboggan cap. It was now about 20°F. outside and Dean and I said *goodnight* while there was still a little light in the western sky. Sleep did not come easily as I tossed and turned in anticipation of 11 p.m., some five hours away.

At 11 p.m., I heard Atilio say, "All right, get up. It's our big day. Washie, washie," with a pan of hot water placed outside the tent.

No "Mzungukichaa!" came out of Dean this morning. It was all seriousness, as if we were all going into battle. We assembled like soldiers promptly in the mess tent and shared some hot tea and cookies without much conversation. The small talk, jokes and laughter had now gone far away. We assembled with backpacks, water, and trekking poles exactly at midnight.

Tosha started leading the twelve of us along with six other guides and a number of porters that could be helpful in case of an emergency. Atilio was carrying my backpack with two liters of water and some extra snacks, and I was carrying two bottles of water inside my jacket, to keep them from freezing, and plenty of M&M peanuts of all sorts of colors. As we climbed and climbed what seemed straight up, I just followed Dean in front of me with my head light on his zig-zagging feet as we continued upward.

After what seemed a couple of hours, Tosha stopped at a wide place in the path. I looked what seemed straight up into the clear sky and located two bright stars at least at eleven o'clock high. As I watched these stars, I saw them start to move and realized it was another group of climbers further up the mountain. That is when I thought to myself, *No way could that be possible. How in the world could that be real, for it was nearly straight up and that is where we must climb.*

The guides told us that one of the main reasons for starting the climb at midnight is to get up to the top of the crater so we could see the sun rise over the horizon. That has always been my vision since I first started planning this climb, but now, I thought to myself, *If it were daylight and we were trying to make this climb, it would be so steep and intimidating that no one would even attempt it, so I guess it was good that it was dark and we couldn't see what was ahead of us.*

After a short rest and plenty of ice cold water, we continued on upward and upward. We made a couple of additional rest stops, and that is when I lay back on a flat rock. Atilio quickly came over and said to me, "Raise up. You can't do that, for you could freeze to death and your body will get lazy, so lean back against my pack." He was bracing it for me with his leg. I accepted his help and encouragement gratefully.

Within five minutes, we moved on forward. The stars were the brightest I have ever seen, but most of my time was spent carefully watching where that I was stepping. A fall or twisted ankle could now be life-threatening. After another couple of hours of exhaustive climbing, I heard someone say, "Be careful, we are now at Gilman's Point."

For me, it was a total surprise to now be at Gilman's Point. I looked at my watch and it was 5:45 a.m. as I stepped on that sacred plateau with the engraved words as shown in the following photograph. I heard the small chatter of a few of the group that had arrived as Atilio was pouring Dean and me a hot cup of tea. The first photograph taken by Dean was of me resting with my back against a rock. As you can tell, I was exhausted.

First photograph after reaching Gilman's Point at about 5:45 a.m. on January 15, 2010 (The date on photograph still shows USA time and camera clock had not yet adjusted itself.)

I took a photograph of Dean resting at Gilman's Point with a hot cup of tea provided by Atilio. Dean shows his exhaustion as well and the twenty below zero temperature.

Dean and I then sat down together in front of that famous Gilman's Point sign for our first photograph taken by Atilio at 5681 meters (18,834 feet.)

Dean having a cup of hot tea after reaching Gilman's Point

Dean and me resting at Gilman's Point with a hot cup of tea from Atillo at 5:45 a.m. on January 15, 2010. Elevation of 5681 meters (18,634 feet)

Dean and I rested for about 10 minutes. We both looked and felt OK—not great, but strong enough to continue. My breathing had become more shallow and rapid as I could feel the cold air fighting for space in my lungs. I knew that I was feeling some tightness in my chest but I had expected that and felt the tightness was normal for this altitude. I evaluated myself as best that I could to be sure that I could walk steady and think clearly which I could.

Dean said, "Uncle Dick, are you going to make it to the summit?"

I said, "Dean, I will make it but maybe a little behind you."

Dean started off following Tosha and a few others. Atilio stayed with me, and in a few minutes, he said to me, "Babu, are you ready to go?" and then he added in a powerful determined voice a phrase that I had never heard him say before, "Let's kick this mountain!"

I replied with just as determined a look, "Let's do it."

Soon we had traversed the snow-covered path of the rim of the crater and could now see the sun coming over the horizon of the earth near Stella's Point. If you stayed at Gilman's point, you never would see this site of the sunrise because you are on the west side of the mountain. In my seventy years, I have seen a lot of beautiful sunrises, but never one like I was seeing, as shown in the following photograph, where it seemed that you could see the curvature of the earth.

01/14/2010

Sunrise on January 15, 2010, near Kilimanjaro's Stella's Point

As we approached Stella's Point, I took another five-minute break with Atilio now becoming my own personal guide and photographer. The glaciers on Mount Kilimanjaro were now in full view. These impressive ice structures date back to the last ice age. As many know, there is a lot of controversy now about the melting or the growing of the glaciers. Atilio said that during his five years of climbing this mountain, he had noticed a major shrinking of the glaciers.

Taking a brief five-minute break at Stella's Point on the way to the summit at Uhuru Peak, now less than an hour away

CHAPTER 6

The Climb to the Summit of Mount Kilimanjaro

Atilio said, "Let's go, Babu, can't let those legs get lazy now."

So off we went at a very slow pace. I am sure as we progressed, I sounded to Atilio like a small child saying, "How much further." He would always say, "Just over that next ridge."

I never thought we would get there. I was more shuffling my feet forward than actual walking. I tried to pick up the pace, but my body wanted no part of that at that altitude. We were slowly making progress, and that is when Atilio put his arm around by back with a steady push forward as we walked.

I felt a little helpless but kept moving forward until we turned the last bend in the path and I could see the summit some fifty yards ahead. I spotted Dean along with a large group of about twenty different climbers already at the summit. These climbers saw me coming, for Dean had already told them that I was his uncle and trying to reach the summit at 70 years old.

These climbers, some in our group but others from another group, formed two lines on each side of the path to the summit. Atilio dropped his arm from my back and said to me, "Babu, you got it made now."

The fellow climbers started to clap for me as I walked forward to meet Dean waiting at the summit of Uhuru Peak. I almost broke down and started to cry, but I still had a few more yards to go and, with adrenaline flowing, I made it as shown in the following photograph.

After controlling my emotions, we had Atilio take a picture of Dean and me at the summit. I still had enough sense to pull open my down jacket to show my Banner Elk Winery shirt, and Dean showed off his Coal Powered t-shirt in support of the Virginia Coal Industry. I had wanted to take a bottle of Banner Elk Wine to the summit but it was too heavy and dangerous, so that idea got left in the USA and the t-shirt had to do.

Dean and me at the summit of Kilimanjaro at Uhuri Peak at 5895 meters (19,341 feet) at 8 a.m. on January 15, 2010

At the summit with my coach and friend, Atilio Hemedi

I also had Dean take my picture with Atilio, my friend and new African son. Without his encouragement and guidance, I feel sure that I could not have made it to the summit. I know that Atilio was just as happy for me as I was, for he took pride in seeing his student not give up and make it to the "Roof of Africa."

Even though the sun was bright and somewhat warm on our faces, the cold air, now about -20°F., was starting to set in on my lungs as I took rapid breaths and started to cough. I knew that I could not stay much longer than five minutes at the summit. Atilio, Dean and I then started back down the same path that we had just climbed.

On our way back to Gilman's Point, I took a lot more notice of the surroundings and the glaciers, now that I had reached my goal. I did not feel so tired, for it was certainly easier walking down than up. It is without doubt, the summit experience and those fellow climbers cheering me on to the finish line that makes this entire experience strangely surreal. The bright sunlight played tricks on the ice and glaciers and the thin air played tricks on my mind and lungs.

As we continued to walk, slowing down by Stella's Point, Atilio took one last photograph of Dean and me standing in front of a giant glacier as shown below.

Dean and me in front of the glaciers near Stella's Point

The magnitude of the moment and the feeling of seeing something that a select few have ever seen are shown all over our faces. In fact, I look a lot better than I felt at that moment. The sights were so beautiful, that I just could not miss a moment. Dean and I had to walk closer to one of the largest glaciers in order to really appreciate the height and magnitude of this moment in earth's history.

A closer look at the glacier at Stella's Point

Coming down may not be as tough as going up, but it did provide its own set of difficulties. Dean continued to move downward at a faster pace, and I told him that I would see him at the base camp at Kibo Hut. It had taken the best that I had to get to the summit and a full eight hours of climbing. Now it was going to take even more to get back down those steep slopes that I first saw at night coming up and thought they were stars rather than climbers above me.

As Atilio and I progressed across the snow-covered edge of the crater's rim approaching Gilman's Point, I began to realize just how dangerous that small path was and could now see it for the first time. If you would fall, you would certainly slide to your death and possible burial site at the bottom of that ice-covered crater as shown in the following two photographs.

01/15/2010

The ice covered path above the crater rim
leaving Gilman's Point to the summit

This snow and ice-covered rim between Gilman's Point and the eastern side of the mountain towards Stella's Point is one of the most treacherous areas on the mountain. One certainly needs to be steady on your feet and using trekking poles before climbing from Gilman's Point to the summit. Again, I was glad that it was still dark when I made the climb earlier. Now that I could see, it gave me cold chills to think of the consequences if one would slip or stumble because of Acute Mountain Sickness or becoming dizzy. Without doubt, Mount Kilimanjaro crater would become your burial site as it has for others who have fallen to their death and are now frozen in time.

The crater rim between Gilman's and Stella's Point
covered in frozen ice and snow

When Atilio and I got back to Gilman's point, Atilio once again pulled out his Maasai Shuka and gave it to me to wrap around my shoulders as congratulations and maybe good luck for getting back off this mountain. I could now see the beauty of this place in full daylight as well as appreciate just how hallowed a place this mountain really is that is called Mount Kilimanjaro.

*Atilio's Maasai Shuka given to me once again on
our return back to Gilman's Point*

I am not sure of all the personal meaning of why Atilio carried his Maasai Shuka to the summit, but to wrap me once again in his Shuka had special significance to him and to me. It sure gave me confidence that we could safely get back off this mountain no matter how long it took. I gave it back after his presentation and photograph. Once again, Atilio folded it carefully, placed it back in his backpack and I never saw it again.

We then proceeded to climb back down among the rocks and followed much of the steep slope and path that we had climbed up some few hours earlier. I began to now, for the first time, realize just how difficult the climb to Gilman's Point was in the earlier hours of the morning. I tried to stop to adjust my boots tighter but I could still feel my feet crushing my toes inside the front part of my boots. The photographs below show the steepness of the slopes and the difficulty after just walking ten hours to the summit and now back to Gilman's Point.

Coming down from Gilman's Point and adjusting boots

I was certainly taking my time, resting in the sun. It was well below zero, though it did not seem that cold. The trekking poles were a must on the way down and crossing the ice fields between Gilman's Point and the summit. I tried to soak in the views of the mountain every chance that I could get to take a breather, but I could tell my lungs were filling up with fluid and each breath was shallower. I knew that it was important for me to keep descending to catch a breath of thicker air. The further we went down, the better I felt, but I still could not catch a deep breath for even as hard as I tried, I would end up coughing mucous from my lungs. I have always had difficulty with sinus infections and drainage, so I knew what it was to cough, which I was now doing frequently. Atilio became a little concerned, but I told him it was OK, for I did not see any blood in the mucous, and I knew as long as the phlegm was loose and I could cough it up that I would be all right.

I took several more stops along the way and could now see Kibo Hut far down the mountain. Atilio and I were sitting down to rest. All of a sudden, Atilio jumped up and said, "Watch out! Here comes a boulder!"

It came rolling down the mountain from way above. This boulder was at least three feet around and gaining speed as it streaked past us to the left and continued on down until it hit a massive boulder and broke apart into smaller rocks that then continued rolling. Atilio said that several people had been killed by such boulders, and it is one of the big hazards on this mountain. I then began to try to move downward more rapidly and with more determination, realizing this was not just another Sunday stroll down any mountainside: this was, after all, Mount Kilimanjaro. I even tried to scree-ski directly down the slope on the loose and fine size volcanic rocks but ended up scooting more on my butt than skiing as shown in the photograph below. After sliding a few more times on my butt, Atilio said, "Let's try skiing together," so he put his arm around my waist and I put my arm around his shoulder. We both scree-skied down together for several thousand feet without falling.

Atilio and I together were able to make great progress downwards. Of all the pictures that I took climbing and descending the mountain, the one picture that I have only in my mind is Atilio and I hugging each other and scree-skiing down that slope together. Here in my mind are two men: a young black man in a yellow jacket and a older white man

Trying to scree-ski down the slope in order to get to a lower elevation faster

with gray hair in a red jacket holding each other arm and arm sliding together down the steep slopes of Mount Kilimanjaro. If I could paint, that is the one picture that I would paint, for that image will always stay in my mind.

To me, that is what this world is all about: embracing each other in a loving and caring relationship with a person whom you may never have met before or may never meet again. Life is all about living peacefully together and helping each other through these various obstacles of life. Living together, peacefully and helping each other, is not a job, it is a human responsibility.

When we got near Kibo Hut, it seemed as if we had been on that mountain for hours. I thought it was about three in the afternoon, and the rest of the camp had left us, for I could see no one milling around the camp. But then again, I looked at my watch and it was just after noon. So it had only taken us four hours to come back from the summit, but it seemed forever. As I got closer to Kibo Hut, I really started to pick up the pace as shown in the following photograph. I was beginning to step high once again even though my feet and toes were feeling a lot of pain.

Stepping high once again as I approached the base camp at Kibo Hut

I looked in my tent, and there was Dean, lying on his sleeping bag sound asleep. The others in the group were also taking a restful nap before having a small spot of hot tea and a box lunch. We all knew we had another five hours of walking to our next campsite, No. 5 at Horombo Bivouac. Because Atilio and I were late arriving, we only had time for some hot tea and to finish packing our gear for the porters, before we had to start walking again. We did not have time to lie down or rest other than sitting down for a cup of hot tea.

The group was soon ready to start out again across the *Saddle*, but taking the Marangu Route to the right rather than the Rongai Route to the left. A friend of Atilio and another guide joined us as we started out a little behind the main group, and we continued at a slightly slower pace. The trek down to Horombo Hut Campsite was not as difficult, for it seemed that I was gaining strength with each step downward. Also, the best part of this route was that the path was wide and I did not have to watch every step that I took. I could now relax and enjoy the view. I started to take deeper breaths, which felt good to my lungs, even though we were still well above 13,000 feet. The photograph on the next page shows the Marangu path to the right side of the Mawenzi Volcano.

I was tired but relaxed, as I was now enjoying going over within the quiet solitude of my mind what I had just achieved. Atilio and the other guide were walking behind, talking and enjoying each other. I was enjoying being by myself as I strolled along even though I was as exhausted as I have ever been. The sun was warm, and in fact hot, on the right side of my face, so much so that I had to put a bandanna under my hat to protect my face from becoming more sunburned. It seemed that we would never get to our next camp at Horombo Hut. But surely, we did finally arrive in about five hours from when we started at Kibo Hut, accounting for a total of seventeen hours of climbing and hiking that day.

Relaxed walking along the descending Marangu Route passing to the right side of the Mawenzi Volcano after climbing to the summit of Mount Kiimanjaro

Day 6: January 16, 2010
Horombo Bivouac at 3720 meters (12,200 feet)

When we got to our campsite, I found Dean chatting it up with other members of the group and then found our tent. It was about 5 p.m. and we had been climbing and walking now for over seventeen hours since we started the summit climb at midnight. Dean had already folded out the sleeping bags and our packs in the tent. I thought just how nice it was that he had taken such good care on this entire trip of his uncle. I told Dean that I was going to bed, not going to have dinner, and for him to work out the arrangements with the others for paying the porters and guides the next morning at the farewell ceremony. This event is always scheduled for the final morning before leaving camp for the final walk to the Marangu Trailhead.

I took an antibiotic and then fell asleep. I slept the best that I had during the entire trip. You might say that I went to bed hungry and woke up happy. I did not even know when Dean came to bed, but I know he was exhausted as well.

The next morning, we all assembled for breakfast, and I had to ask Dean what was the agreed amount of tip to give to the support team. All twelve members agreed to give the maximum recommended as tip, for indeed the total services organized by the African Walking Company were excellent. While I was sleeping and not at dinner to protect myself, the group had nominated me to make the final farewell speech and to pass out the agreed-upon funding for the support team. During my walk the afternoon before and during my sleep, I had already thought out what I was going to do and say particularly to Atilio in front his peers. The entire team of twelve climbers and 36 support team members, ranging from cooks, porters, to guides were all at this ritual ceremony as shown in the following photograph.

It was cold that morning but sunny. The temperature was below freezing, but with the excitement around breakfast, the entire camp was buzzing with a feeling of happiness. We were still above 12,200 feet in elevation. At this ritual ceremony, the entire support team thanked us for coming to see and climb their mountain. They, as a team, sang a song to us which we recorded and which was very dear. Then the chief

*The assembly of the twelve climbers and 36 support team at
the ritual ceremony on the morning of January 16, 2010*

guide, Tosha Minja, made a statement to our entire group of twelve
climbers. His statement had a profound meaning to all of us, for he
said, "Climbers, all twelve of you, I have been climbing this mountain
for more than ten years and we have never before had the entire team of
twelve reach Gilman's Point and eleven of you made it to the summit.
Also, 'Babu Wolfe' is the oldest person that I have witnessed reaching the
summit at Uhura Point, so he has set the bar for all of us. I congratulate
you as a team, for you all pulled together as a unified group, and that
makes all the difference in the total climb."

In turn, I had the opportunity to speak on behalf of the entire
group of climbers and expressed our appreciation for all that they had
done for each of us and together. I personally expressed my appreciation
for all the support granted me and their help in my climbing to the
summit at 70 years old. They gave me applause, out of respect for the
achievement, which touched my heart.

I passed out the maximum tips recommended by the group to the
chief guide, Tosha, for his distribution to his entire staff. I then made a
personal presentation to Atilio Hemedi emphasizing all that he had done
for me throughout the climb and named him my coach and "African
son." I gave him my Banner Elk Winery Shirt and Hat that I wore to
the summit along with a major special tip. Everyone in the group gave
Atilio a special recognition and applause.

We were soon off as a group walking down the Marangu route which was a wide, well- marked trail. We had another eleven miles to go to the Marangu Trailhead and the awaiting vehicles. The toes on both of my feet were bruised and hurting from the steep descent, and it was painful to walk even at a slow pace. Still, I was absorbing as much of the beauty and the environment as I could, and I was not in any big hurry.

The descending trail not far from our camp is shown in the following photograph. Atilio told me that this was the location that was used during the filming of the famous movie, *Snows of Kilimanjaro,* that started me on this adventure some 53 years earlier.

The final trail coming from the Horombut Hut Campsite with Mount Kilimanjaro barely visible in the background. This was the same location use in filming the famous movie in 1952 called "Snows of Kilimanjaro" starring Gregory Peck, Susan Hayward, and Ava Gardner and written by Ernest Hemingway.

One might expect that an adventurer like Ernest Hemingway would have visited Kilimanjaro. No doubt he did, and that is where he got his inspiration to write the famous short story, "Snows of Kilimanjaro," in 1936. To me, this place had a special meaning too, for it was when I ran the projectors in our local theater in Sophia, West Virginia, back in 1957 that I first heard of Mount Kilimanjaro.

My breathing and chest were now feeling better even though I was still coughing. The night before, I had taken a couple of antibiotics that Dr. Zuber had given me before the trip as a precaution. I felt sure these antibiotics would help break up the sinus congestion as would getting into thicker air. We were now descending from a height of 12,200 feet to an elevation of 5900 feet at the Marangu Trailhead.

The Marangu Route is the most popular route to the mountain base camp at Kibo Hut and is wide and well-marked. In addition, travelling on this route, the climbers stay in wooden huts with about twenty beds with special dividers installed, along with a real "out house" toilets. This is the route that President Jimmy Carter took in 1988 to the Kibo Hut. I am sure President Carter took this route because of security purposes and to accommodate his own support group of physicians and security personnel. For our indomitable troupe, the route was our reward for taking the most difficult route up to the summit of Kilimanjaro.

No doubt, the Marangu Route is a much easier walking and climbing route than the Rongai Route to the Base Camp at Kibo Hut. But no matter which route gets you to that base camp, everyone has to make the summit climb, which is by far the most difficult of all the climbs. Without doubt, Kilimanjaro saves its most grueling trail for the last leg of the journey to the summit, so that all who make the trek appreciate their rejuvenating time at Kibo Hut.

Our trek through the rain forest, as shown in the following photograph, went rather quickly as I became fascinated by the different flowers and the beautiful butterflies. We saw several monkeys and a large number of beautiful birds. I felt also, this would be a great place as a home for some large leopard to hide out, but apparently there are no such animals in this part of the Kilimanjaro National Park.

Being an amateur butterfly collector who had collected many butterflies during my training hikes around Banner Elk, North Carolina, I tried to catch a few with my hat on the way down. I was able to catch one beautiful specimen as shown in the following photograph. I carefully pressed the butterfly in a small book that I was carrying and now have it mounted on my wall in my office in Banner Elk. Trying to catch butterflies became a joy and Atilio joined in the fun, but had no luck. I remarked to him that some of the village kids could make a nice income by catching and selling some of their lovely butterflies like they do in Brazil and other countries. Maybe that opportunity will catch on by some enterprising young boy or girl.

*The rain forest as we descended along the Marangu
Route towards the gate at the Marangu Trailhead*

*An example of the many beautiful butterflies seen
along the Marangu Route*

The final few miles were very pleasant and Atilio and I talked most of the way about his life and what he wanted to do in the future. We had truly become friends, and I feel sure that he will never forget me nor will I ever forget him. As we finally came in view of the gate, some one hour later than most of the group, we passed the most famous monument of Hans Meyer who was the first European explorer who conquered the summit of Mount Kilimanjaro in 1889.

Monument to Hans Meyer at the Marangu Trailhead.

As I read the words on this monument, I began to wonder what African climbed that summit first and how he did it without all the proper clothing and gear. For I know now what a challenge it is to scale Kilimanjaro to the summit. I am thrilled to have finally achieved that one adventure on my "Bucket List" even though it took me seventy years to do it. However, I am always reminded of what my dad would tell me, "Son remember that the turtle did not get on the fence post by itself," and neither did I make it to summit by myself.

From the day one at the Rongai Trailhead leading up to Mount Kilimanjaro and returning to Marangu Trailhead, we had walked a total of at least fifty miles.

Day 7: January 17, 2010
Moivaro Lodge in Arusha, Tanzania

After leaving the gate and saying goodbye to all our guides and porters, and especially to Atilio, we boarded the van to travel several more hours, first to pick up our leftover supplies at the Kilimanjaro Mountain Resort and to travel on as a group to where we were all staying the last night at the beautiful Moivaro Lodge. We all quickly checked in and then made our way to the rooms for a hot shower. The various cottages were located around a lovely swimming pool and the central lodge was nestled among the banana trees as shown in the following photograph.

Moivaro Lodge where we spent the final night after coming off the mountain

We each rested in our own way, and then some of us gathered before dinner in the bar to share a cold beer named "Kilimanjaro." Dean and I toasted each other with a renewed smile of gratification as shown in the following photograph. One might say in a small way, "This was our Olympic Trial and we both won a gold medal."

*Dean and I toasting each other with a cold beer
called "Kilimanjaro"*

That evening we had a lovely dinner, and the entire group sat in amazement as the final talks and certificates were handed out by our elected presenter, Mr. Graham Mitchell from England. After Graham had given all the certificates out, he did not have one for himself and he said, "Did any of you have two certificates—for I don't have one?" Of course, you might guess by now, "Mzungukichaa" had already been at work and removed Graham's certificate from the group. After a few minutes, Graham was greatly relieved and pleased to have his certificate presented to him by Dean.

A copy of my certificate is shown in the following paragraph. This certificate is now mounted on my office wall along with my most prized possessions including my diplomas for my earned BS, MS and Ph.D. degrees from two universities.

We all said our goodbyes to one another, hoping to meet again. About five of the group were now heading off for a five-day Safari in the Serengeti. That safari was indeed another adventure of itself and allowed Dean and me both the opportunity to recuperate from our climb.

MOUNT KILIMANJARO-TANZANIA

Senecio kilimanjari	● Uhuru Peak (UP) 5895 m ● Stella Point (SP) 5756 m ● Gilman's Point (GP) 5685 m	Impatiens kilimanjari

This is to certify that

Mr / Mrs / Miss ___RICHARD WOLFE___

has successfully climbed Mt. Kilimanjaro the Highest in

Africa to **Uhuru Peak 5895m** amsl

Date...15 – 1 – 2010... Time...8:00 AM... Age...70 YRS...

TOSHA MINJA

GUIDE   **CHIEF PARK WARDEN**   **DIRECTOR GENERAL**

Kilimanjaro National Park   Tanzania National Parks

CERTIFICATE No. UP .....81461.........

Certificate awarded to Richard Wolfe for climbing to Uhuru Peak at 19,341 feet, the summit of Mount Kilimanjaro arriving on January 15, 2010, at 8:00 a.m.

Summary of the Climb
to the Roof of Africa

What started 53 years ago as a vision in my head when I first heard the word "Kilimanjaro" in the famous movie, *Snows of Kilimanjaro*, now has become a reality in my soul. I achieved an adventurous climb at 70 years old to the summit of Kilimanjaro that was more difficult and challenging than I had ever imagined. For me, it was as mentally challenging as it was physically, particularly that last leg of the journey from Gilman's Point to the summit at Uhura Peak.

In retrospect, if I had not gone beyond Gilman's Point, I would have missed the most amazing part of the entire climb. To see the sun rise over the curvature of the earth and to observe those beautiful glaciers that have existed for millions of years were the most inspiring part of the entire climb up to the summit of Mount Kilimanjaro.

All in all, this trip could not have gone any better from start to finish. The African Walking Company did an outstanding job of scheduling and arranging the entire trip.

As for medications, I took my blood pressure and cholesterol pills, and a baby aspirin each day and took medicine as a preventive drug for Acute Mountain Sickness after reaching an elevation above 10,000 feet. Dean, along with a couple of others, did not take the preventive drug for AMS.

The youngest member of the group was a girl of 25 who had just finished her Master's Degree at Oxford University in England. It turned out that I was 45 years older than the youngest member of our group and seventeen years older than the second-eldest member who was Dr. Hoopman from Australia. The last day before leaving camp, Dean and I both started taking a pill for preventing malaria. We were planning to spend the next five days resting and recovering on a Safari in the Serengeti and knew we might be exposed to mosquitoes carrying the malaria disease which is bad in Tanzania.

As for the proper clothes to wear at the summit, I had learned during the winters in Banner Elk, North Carolina, and while hunting at temperatures below zero, that one must not wear cotton clothing but polyester moisture-wicking underwear, sweaters, and socks. Glove liners under ski gloves were a must as well as sock liners and wicking socks like Thoros®. Good boots that are water-proof with good soles are essential. Your feet are your wheels on this climb and you need to pay then special attention. The lightweight, down-filled jacket with a hood that I rented was excellent. I needed a face mask to breathe through to help warm the air before going into my lungs. However, the mask made my glasses fog up, and I finally had to forgo the face mask because it was more important for me to see where I was walking. The only injury that I suffered from the climb was the bruised toes that occurred during the steep descent.

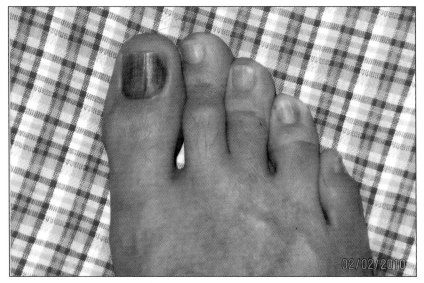

Bruised big toe from descending the steep slopes of Mount Kilimanjaro
(What a small price to pay for such an adventure!)

I feel sure that living in Banner Elk, North Carolina, at 4300 feet and climbing daily upon Beech Mountain at 5500 feet for more than a year was a major factor in preventing me from getting Acute Mountain Sickness on the climb. Also, those daily climbs got me in the best physical and mental condition that I have ever been and gave me the strength to climb to the summit of Mount Kilimanjaro at my age of 70.

It was an awesome journey to the roof of Africa. However, I could not have made it without the personal coaching and guidance from Atilio Hemedi. This young man is certainly my hero and gave me a nickname of "Babu," which I am extremely proud of and will stay with me forever. I would recommend Atilio and the chief guide, Tosha Minja, along with the African Walking Company, to anyone considering a trip to climb Mount Kilimanjaro.

I know the African tradition states than only those who have climbed to the summit can refer to Mount Kilimanjaro as *Kili*. I suppose that I have earned that right but now after experiencing the magnitude and difficulty of that climb to the summit, I feel it is disrespectful to call that mountain anything other than Mount Kilimanjaro. Just because one may have climbed that mountain once, that is no guarantee that you can climb it again. I believe the mountain gods were kind to me, for we caught the mountain calm with clear skies and only a little wind. I know that I am thankful that the full fury of Mount Kilimanjaro never showed itself to me on January 15, 2010, for it was tough enough the way it was for a man of 70.

—*Dick Wolfe*

**Coming in 2011!
by Dick Wolfe**

Watch for ...

HIGH COUNTRY IS WINE COUNTRY

Wine making is both an art and a science:
❧ It's about subtlety and nuance.
❧ It's about knowledge of the climate, of specific site character-istics, of the viticulture practices and winemaking techniques.
❧ It's about achieving a unique character and complexity in each wine produced.
❧ Crafting and creating a fine wine is not simply an occupa-tion. It is a passion.

Dr. Wolfe demonstrates that wines from grapes grown at higher el-evations around the world produce the highest quality wines. French vintnors have demonstrated that the grapes that slowly ripen and stay on the vines longer have the best opportunity to benefit from the full mineral content and composition of the soil, thus adding to the over-all quality of the wine. The author discusses "The French Paradox." the health benefits of red wine from a scientific standpoint.

The author also relates how the wine industry started in the High Country of North Carolina in 2001 and why this area may become the wine capital of the east.

Visit our website: www.bannerelkwinery.com.

Mountain Empire resident scales Mount Kilimanjaro on 70th birthday

By Michael L. Owens
Bristol Herald Courier
February 1, 2010

Richard Wolfe didn't care about the air's icy bite: It was fresh—the purest he'd ever inhaled.

So what if a battle raged in his lungs—as the thin, mountain air fought for space against a dangerous fluid build-up? It took nearly a week of day-long hikes and nights in a sleeping bag to reach this point. He couldn't turn back now, not with the peak of Mount Kilimanjaro finally in sight.

Wolfe's pace slowed as he neared the 19,341-foot summit—more like shuffling forward than actual walking. Debilitating headaches and nonstop vomiting already had convinced others in the group to turn back. But Wolfe continued upward, determined to reach Africa's highest peak.

Never mind that climbers have roughly five minutes to admire the serenity before more-severe symptoms of altitude sickness set in.

Despite the danger, Wolfe just had to push forward. Celebrating his 70th birthday any other way was out of the question.

Getting there

Coal is how Wolfe is best known.

Though he operates a vineyard in Banner Elk, N.C., it is his search for clean-coal technology in Southwest Virginia that has grabbed local headlines in recent years.

Next on his to-do list is to write a book about his adventure, titled "Climbing Kilimanjaro at 70."

"I want to set the bar, maybe, for others at 70," Wolfe said. "I want to let people know it can be done."

Wolfe is not the oldest person to scale the inactive volcano in northeastern Tanzania, on the eastern side of the continent. In fact, there's a bit of contention over who holds that record, according to Climb Mount Kilimanjaro.com.

The Guinness Book of World Records bestows the distinction upon American Carl Haupt, who was 79 years old when he reached the top in 2004.

But many Web sites dedicated to the mountain credit a Frenchman named Valtee Daniel as the oldest at 87, according to Climb Mount Kilimanjaro.com. None of the sites say when Daniel reached the top.

Wolfe's first night on Kilimanjaro was Jan. 11—his 70th birthday.

Joining him was his nephew Dean Yates, 36, of Abingdon, Va.

"Physically, it was the hardest thing I've ever endured in my life," Yates said of the hike to the top. "There was headaches at the base of my head, there was queasiness... I didn't train enough."

Yates decided against taking any medicine for altitude sickness.

"I just wanted to see if my body could acclimate to it," he said.

Wolfe, on the other hand, embraced the medication.

Just setting foot on the mountain took several days of hiking through a 95-degree rainforest. So it wasn't a matter of parking the car at the base and emptying the truck of camping supplies.

Wolfe and Yates were among a 24-person tour group comprised of Russians, Australians, more Americans and a British special forces soldier.

Even more tour guides accompanied them.

"This was an expedition," Wolfe said. "This is not something you can do on your own."

After decades of dreaming, Wolfe had finally made it to the starting point. In four more days, he would reach his goal.

And it was more than just a whim that brought him to this point.

Wolfe spent the previous year hiking the mountains of North Carolina in preparation. There also were a slew of medical exams.

"At 70, I needed to know if I could make it," Wolfe said.

The prep work might have started then, but the dream began 53 years ago.

Dream

An upbringing in West Virginia's coalfields fueled Wolfe's passion for coal-based technology. It also set him on the path to Kilimanjaro.

As a teenager, Wolfe manned the projectors at the town movie theater. That's where a lifelong mission began to take shape, born the moment the 1952 classic "The Snows of Kilimanjaro" splashed onto the theater's screen.

Staring Gregory Peck, the movie is based on the short story of the same name by Ernest Hemingway.

"I?ve thought about that mountain since I was 17 years old," Wolfe said.

Decades later, he can now hold aloft a certificate bearing his name and signed by both the warden of Kilimanjaro National Park and the director of Tanzania National Parks.

Wolfe reached the summit at 8 a.m. Jan. 15, 2010, the certificate proclaims.

The certificate means that Wolfe stood above glaciers thousands of years old as he touched the sky.

"It's super quiet," Wolfe said of a serenity he had never before experienced. "And, going up there, I've never seen stars so bright."

Onward and upward

Frostbite ate at the fingers of one of the Australians.

Others in the expedition suffered from pain and vomiting, despite the meds for altitude sickness.

"When we first got to the base of our trail, there was some woman from another tour group coming back down and she said to just turn around now," Yates recalled.

Travel is done at a snail's pace. The average human body can take but only so much torture.

"You go as slow as you can physically walk," Wolfe said. "It's as slow as you've ever moved."

Of course, the tour guides scaled the mountains with ease.

Having made the climb many times before, some guides slipped ahead of the tourists near the end of each day to set camp.

And each tourist retreat back down the mountain meant a guide was freed to act as personal aide for a hiker.

With Wolfe, that guide was Atilio Hemedi. He called Wolfe babu, which is Swahili for grandfather.

"My guide, he kept encouraging me," Wolfe said. "He was my African son."

Kilimanjaro saves its most gruelling trail for the last leg of the journey.

The peak is reached only after a six-hour trek along an almost vertical trail.

"It's as much mental as it is physical," Wolfe said of meeting the challenge.

Yates scaled the trail ahead of Wolfe. He wanted to be there to welcome his uncle.

Near the journey's end, Wolfe wondered if his legs could carry him the last few yards. That?s when his fellow hikers already at the top erupted with applause.

"They started clapping for me," Wolfe said. "I believe that was enough adrenaline to get me up there."

Wolfe on Kilimanjaro

By Frank Ruggiero
The Mountain Times
March 18, 2010

Like most adventures, Dick Wolfe's started in a cinema.

A noted chemist, Wolfe is known locally as the vintner and co-owner of the award-winning Banner Elk Winery. But 53 years ago, he was running a movie projector in Sophia, W.Va.

The film was The Snows of Kilimanjaro, starring Gregory Peck and Susan Hayward, based on Ernest Hemingway's short story.

"That was my eyes to the world," Wolfe said of the cinema, "and the first time I'd heard of Kilimanjaro. You have a quest sometimes, when you think, 'I can do this, and I can do that.' Mt. Kilimanjaro has always been mine since I was a teenager."

Decades later, Wolfe celebrated his 70th birthday in Tanzania, specifically Uhuru Peak, the highest summit of Mt. Kilimanjaro, at 19,341 feet above sea level — the tallest mountain in Africa, and the tallest freestanding mountain in the world.

"Like so many things, growing up in these (Appalachian) mountains gave me the chance to get to know these mountains," said Wolfe, who, as a child, would race 4 to 5 miles up and down the slopes. "I guess I've been preparing myself all my life."

The more intensive preparation came this past year, namely by hiking weekly to the summits of area slopes in Banner Elk and Beech Mountain, what Wolfe called "one of the better training grounds" for mountain ascensions.

Meanwhile, Wolfe's nephew, landscaper and Virginia Tech graduate Dean Yates, 36, who would accompany him on the expedition, trained in Abingdon, Va. Though nearly overwhelmed by Kilimanjaro's harsh climate, both were fully prepared, as were the 14 others in their 24-person expedition, divided into two groups, who achieved the summit.

Wolfe and Yates were the only two Americans in the group, others hailing from the United Kingdom, Australia and relatively flat locales.

"They'd hiked, but there's a difference between hiking and climbing," Wolfe said. "It turns out I'm a better climber than a hiker."

The journey to the top was 50 miles, 25 up and 25 back to the gate of Kilimanjaro National Park. Wolfe said it takes four days to just reach the base camp, though it was anything but an uneventful trip. They started on Jan. 11, Wolfe's birthday, encountering numbers of Tanzanian locals, a colorful variety of wildlife, including monkeys, buffalo and elephants, and remarkable changes in climate.

"You start out in the rainforest — and boy, did it rain — and get higher to the heather, and then the moorland, with mostly volcanic rock and very little vegetation," Wolfe said.

Employing the services of African Walking Company, Wolfe, Yates and company were backed by a 36-person support team of sherpas and auxiliary staff. One of the guides, Atilio Hemedi, took an instant liking to Wolfe, affectionately nicknaming him "Babu," meaning "Grandpa."

"I got to know Atilio really well," Wolfe said. "He told me the same thing my dad told me: I want to give my children a good education, so they don't have to work in these mountains."

Wolfe said his father worked hard in the coal mines of West Virginia, so he wouldn't have to. He and Atilio became fast friends, and he was truly touched when several talented cooks prepared him a birthday cake one evening.

"I was 17 years older than anybody in these two groups," Wolfe said. "Fifty-three was the second oldest age, a doctor from Australia."

The next morning, Wolfe saw Kilimanjaro — in person — for the first time, looming about 18 to 20 miles away. The expedition was told to always follow four golden rules: "Poly-poly," positive attitude, hydration, and climb high, sleep low.

"(The guides) call it 'poly-poly,' which means 'slowly slowly,'" Wolfe said. "Going slow helps you climatize, but it was at a slower pace than I'd practiced."

Before turning in for the night, the group would climb 1,000 feet, and then come back down — climb high, sleep low, thus growing accustomed to the ever-increasing elevation. Upon reaching the Kilimanjaro valley, the altitude was an approximate 12,000 feet. Eight miles later, they reached Kibo Hut, base camp. They ate early that night, around 5, so they could catch several hours' sleep before starting their ascension at 11 p.m.

"We'd already hiked 8 miles through the valley, so we were pretty tired," Wolfe said. "But trying to go to sleep, knowing the quest would start at 11, was difficult. I got the feeling like someone going to battle. It's really hard not to have your adrenaline pumping. I knew it was going to be the most difficult part of the trip."

In this case, difficult equals a 6,500-foot ascent up an increasingly steep grade. The 11 p.m. starting time was set, so the climbers could witness sunrise on the slopes of Kilimanjaro. Wolfe suspects an untold reason is so climbers won't notice the steep slopes quite so much.

"I'd look up and see the stars, what I thought were stars, but they were moving," Wolfe said. "They were the other climbers' lights."

Wolfe reached Gilman's Point, 18,638 feet above sea level, in the early hours of Jan. 15, still quite dark, but just in time to watch the sun rise over the crest, an image he'll not soon forget.

He and his nephew enjoyed a brief reprieve with a cup of hot coffee, before setting out toward Stella Point, only about 300 feet higher, but a grueling 300 feet.

"By now, we're at 20 degrees below zero, and oxygen's about half of what it is here," Wolfe said.

"I was really being honest with myself. I didn't want to die on that mountain. When I got to Gilman's Point, I tried to assess my thoughts. When you don't get as much oxygen to the brain, you get wobbly and can't think straight. I didn't get like that. I could feel my breath shortening, but my guide said, 'You've got to keep going. If you stop, your legs get lazy and you'll freeze up here.'"

Attributing this resilience to his High Country training, Wolfe didn't have much trouble taking Atilio's advice. From Stella Point, the final stop was Uhuru Peak, about 400 vertical feet away, and the uppermost summit on Kilimanjaro's Kibo crater rim, the highest of the mountain's three volcanic cones. Yates had reached the top, with Wolfe about 30 minutes behind. "I was ahead of some, but my guide was right there with me at the end," he said.

Upon reaching the summit's thin air, climbers are urged to spend no more than 15 minutes there for health and safety. Yates stayed 30, waiting for his uncle to arrive.

What Wolfe encountered there brought tears to his eyes.

Along with Yates, his fellow climbers were waiting, clapping as he arrived. Wolfe achieved the summit at 8 a.m. on Jan. 15, an eight-hour journey.

"It was quiet, other than the clapping," he said. "I looked around, had a moment to myself. The air was cold, but crystal clear, and I could see the curvature of the Earth. I got tears in my eyes."

It was 20 below, but the sun was shining, and Wolfe couldn't resist the opportunity to tout his winery, unzipping his jacket to reveal a Banner Elk Winery T-shirt and pose for a photograph.

Wolfe spent the recommended 15 minutes there, before starting the equally, if not more, tricky descent. Upon reaching Gilman's Point the second time, Atilio, of Masai heritage, gave Wolfe his tribal cloth, "So, I was truly his Babu," he said.

The downhill trip past base camp and beyond took a total of 18 hours, and Wolfe slept hard that night, forgoing supper for slumber.

Wolfe still attributes his success on Kilimanjaro to his persistent training on Beech Mountain, claiming the High Country is an ideal training ground for such feats. But Wolfe already had an advantage: Resolve.

"Here I set this goal for myself," he said. "It showed what perseverance could do in anything. I'm not the kind of person to give up."

View from the Top

70-YEAR-OLD SOPHIA NATIVE
CLIMBS MOUNT KILIMANJARO

By Christopher J. Jackson
Register-Herald Reporter
February 28, 2010

BECKLEY — He called it his eyes to the world.

Every day after class, Richard Wolfe spent the remaining hours of the day operating the 35mm film projector at Sophia Theater.

It was in between the film reeling through the gate and the take-up that the Sophia High School senior's eyes saw beyond the rolling mountains of southern West Virginia.

One film in particular that caught his eye was the 1952 film adaptation of Ernest Hemingway's short story "The Snows of Kilimanjaro" staring Gregory Peck.

The year was 1957 and Wolfe was 17 years old. The Henry King film left an indelible impression on Wolfe, so much so that 53 years later, Wolfe scaled Mount Kilimanjaro, the tallest peak in Africa, at the proper age of 70—and on his birthday.

"I was fascinated by that mountain all my life," said Wolfe, who now lives in Banner Elk, N.C. "I've had goals all my life and it's something I'd been working on for a long time."

Wolfe credits growing up in Sophia and living in Banner Elk near Beech Mountain, the highest peak in North Carolina at 5,500 feet, for his ability to climb the fourth-tallest peak in the world at age 70.

"I think the climate is key," he said. "You might have physically enough strength, but you don't know who will get sick because of the altitude—it's thin air, half the oxygen."

He trained daily for a year, walking 2 to 3 miles up Beech Mountain. Before leaving for Tanzania, Wolfe was checked out by a doctor to ensure that his heart was capable of such an arduous task.

Wolfe said he wanted to climb the 19,341-foot mountain on his 70th birthday. He ascended the summit on July 11 — his birthday — and reached it on the early morning of July 15.

Wolfe went with two groups of 12 people and his nephew, Dean Yates, 36. He said he was 20 years older than anyone in his group.

"Fifty percent of people don't make it," he said. "That's what our group was, about 50 percent made it."

They left for Uhuru Peak, the summit, at midnight from their base camp. As he zigged-zagged toward the summit, his group slowly pulled away from him. He looked up and saw the stars, the brightest he had ever seen. He felt his legs slow, his breathing became shallow as his lungs filled with fluid.

"I never had a negative thought," he said. "As long as I could think clearly, I knew I'd make it."

Encouraging words from Atilio Hemedi, one of the guides on the expedition, kept him going. Hemedi stayed with Wolfe during their trek to Uhuru Peak. Wolfe said "without him I don't think I could have made it.

Wolfe reached Gilman's Point, which is where the crater rim begins, while it was still dark.

"You had to walk across craters, you got to be able to walk steady," he said. "I said, 'I might be a little behind you, but I'll make it.'"

Yates asked if he could make it to the summit, and he replied, "I think I can."

Then he saw it.

"The sunrise gave me a lot of exhilaration," he said about reaching the top and seeing the curvature of the earth.

He could see the peak about 50 yards away and about 25 people were there, he said. Yates told the group his uncle was coming and that he's 70. They formed two lines and applauded as he inched forward.

"I almost broke down," he said as the group clapped him on. "It was the toughest, physical and mental, thing I've ever done."

His group didn't stay long at the summit, about 10 minutes at most, he said. Coming back down the mountain he saw for the first time where he had come.

"I could see where I just climbed and it was scary," he said. "I think if I saw that going up it'd be so intimidating I think I'd turned around."

He said it took him about five days to recover from climbing the mountain. He's written a book, titled "Climbing Kilimanjaro at 70," and is seeking a publisher.

Wolfe, the son of a coal miner, grew up loving the mountains and received a coal mining scholarship to Virginia Tech, where he earned his doctorate in engineering.

He says he has dedicated his entire life to clean coal technology and has patented a way to remove mercury from coal before it's burned.

Wolfe has been the director of applied sciences at Appalachian State University and is currently contracted with West Virginia University, where he is working on his patented clean coal technology.

He's also the president of Carbonite Corp.

Wolfe also makes wine at his home in Banner Elk. He said people today can do things at his age that they couldn't do yesterday.

"I've set the bar a little bit," he said. "We can do things at 70—older now than we used to—if we just keep ourselves in good physical condition."

Visit the website for
Banner Elk Winery
& Inn
for more books by

Dr. Dick Wolfe &
the North Carolina High Country's premiere winery

Banner Elk Winery marks the genesis of the wine tradition in the High Country of North Carolina as the first commercial winery built in Avery and Watauga counties. The creations of Vintner Dr. Richard Wolfe pay tribute to the rugged mountain landscape and capture the delicate nuance and character of the fruit. Processing locally grown grapes into excellent wines that reflect the unique characteristics of the Appalachian Mountains, Dr. Wolfe provides guidance and encouragement to local farmers planting vineyards with the new French-American and American varieties of grapes.

www.bannerelkwinery.com